# Rediscovering Psycl

*Rediscovering Psychoanalysis* demonstrates how, by attending to one's own idiosyncratic ways of thinking, feeling, and responding to patients, the psychoanalyst can develop a "style" of his or her own, a way of practicing that is a living process originating, to a large degree, from the personality and experience of the analyst.

This book approaches rediscovering psychoanalysis from four vantage points derived from the author's experience as a clinician, a supervisor, a teacher, and a reader of psychoanalysis. Thomas Ogden begins by presenting his experience of creating psychoanalysis freshly in the form of "talking-as-dreaming" in the analytic session; this is followed by an exploration of supervising and teaching psychoanalysis in a way that is distinctly one's own and unique to each supervisee and seminar group. Ogden goes on to rediscover psychoanalysis in this book as he continues his series of close readings of seminal analytic works. Here, he makes original theoretical contributions through the exploration, explication, and extension of the work of Bion, Loewald, and Searles.

Throughout this text, Thomas Ogden offers ways of revitalizing and reinventing the exchange between analyst and patient in each session, making this book essential reading for psychoanalysts, psychotherapists, and other readers with an interest in psychoanalysis.

**Thomas H. Ogden** is the winner of the 2004 *International Journal of Psychoanalysis* Award for Outstanding Paper. He is the Director of the Center for the Advanced Study of the Psychoses and a member of the International Psychoanalytical Association. His previous publications include *This Art of Psychoanalysis: Dreaming Undreamt Dreams and Interrupted Cries*. His work has been published in 16 languages.

# THE NEW LIBRARY OF PSYCHOANALYSIS

General Editor Dana Birksted-Breen

The New Library of Psychoanalysis was launched in 1987 in association with the Institute of Psychoanalysis, London. It took over from the International Psychoanalytical Library which published many of the early translations of the works of Freud and the writings of most of the leading British and Continental psychoanalysts.

The purpose of the New Library of Psychoanalysis is to facilitate a greater and more widespread appreciation of psychoanalysis and to provide a forum for increasing mutual understanding between psychoanalysts and those working in other disciplines such as the social sciences, medicine, philosophy, history, linguistics, literature and the arts. It aims to represent different trends both in British psychoanalysis and in psychoanalysis generally. The New Library of Psychoanalysis is well placed to make available to the English-speaking world psychoanalytic writings from other European countries and to increase the interchange of ideas between British and American psychoanalysts.

The Institute, together with the British Psychoanalytical Society, runs a low-fee psychoanalytic clinic, organizes lectures and scientific events concerned with psychoanalysis and publishes the *International Journal of Psychoanalysis*. It also runs the only UK training course in psychoanalysis which leads to membership of the International Psychoanalytical Association – the body which preserves internationally agreed standards of training, of professional entry, and of professional ethics and practice for psychoanalysis as initiated and developed by Sigmund Freud. Distinguished members of the Institute have included Michael Balint, Wilfred Bion, Ronald Fairbairn, Anna Freud, Ernest Jones, Melanie Klein, John Rickman, and Donald Winnicott.

Previous General Editors include David Tuckett, Elizabeth Spillius and Susan Budd. Previous and current Members of the Advisory Board include Christopher Bollas, Ronald Britton, Catalina Bronstein, Donald Campbell, Sara Flanders, Stephen Grosz, John Keene, Eglé Laufer, Juliet Mitchell, Michael Parsons, Rosine Jozef Perelberg, Mary Target, and David Taylor, and Richard Rusbridger, who is now Assistant Editor.

ALSO IN THIS SERIES

*Impasse and Interpretation* Herbert Rosenfeld
*Psychoanalysis and Discourse* Patrick Mahony
*The Suppressed Madness of Sane Men* Marion Milner
*The Riddle of Freud* Estelle Roith
*Thinking, Feeling, and Being* Ignacio Matte-Blanco
*The Theatre of the Dream* Salomon Resnik
*Melanie Klein Today: Volume 1, Mainly Theory* Edited by Elizabeth Bott Spillius
*Melanie Klein Today: Volume 2, Mainly Practice* Edited by Elizabeth Bott Spillius
*Psychic Equilibrium and Psychic Change: Selected Papers of Betty Joseph* Edited by Michael Feldman and Elizabeth Bott Spillius
*About Children and Children-No-Longer: Collected Papers 1942–80* Paula Heimann. Edited by Margret Tonnesmann
*The Freud–Klein Controversies 1941–45* Edited by Pearl King and Riccardo Steiner
*Dream, Phantasy and Art* Hanna Segal
*Psychic Experience and Problems of Technique* Harold Stewart
*Clinical Lectures on Klein and Bion* Edited by Robin Anderson
*From Fetus to Child* Alessandra Piontelli
*A Psychoanalytic Theory of Infantile Experience: Conceptual and Clinical Reflections* E. Gaddini. Edited by Adam Limentani
*The Dream Discourse Today* Edited and introduced by Sara Flanders
*The Gender Conundrum: Contemporary Psychoanalytic Perspectives on Feminitity and Masculinity* Edited and introduced by Dana Breen
*Psychic Retreats* John Steiner
*The Taming of Solitude: Separation Anxiety in Psychoanalysis* Jean-Michel Quinodoz
*Unconscious Logic: An Introduction to Matte-Blanco's Bi-logic and its Uses* Eric Rayner
*Understanding Mental Objects* Meir Perlow
*Life, Sex and Death: Selected Writings of William Gillespie* Edited and introduced by Michael Sinason
*What Do Psychoanalysts Want? The Problem of Aims in Psychoanalytic Therapy* Joseph Sandler and Anna Ursula Dreher
*Michael Balint: Object Relations, Pure and Applied* Harold Stewart
*Hope: A Shield in the Economy of Borderline States* Anna Potamianou

*Psychoanalysis, Literature and War: Papers 1972–1995* Hanna Segal
*Emotional Vertigo: Between Anxiety and Pleasure* Danielle Quinodoz
*Early Freud and Late Freud* Ilse Grubrich-Simitis
*A History of Child Psychoanalysis* Claudine and Pierre Geissmann
*Belief and Imagination: Explorations in Psychoanalysis* Ronald Britton
*A Mind of One's Own: A Kleinian View of Self and Object* Robert A. Caper
*Psychoanalytic Understanding of Violence and Suicide* Edited by Rosine Jozef Perelberg
*On Bearing Unbearable States of Mind* Ruth Riesenberg-Malcolm
*Psychoanalysis on the Move: The Work of Joseph Sandler* Edited by Peter Fonagy, Arnold M. Cooper and Robert S. Wallerstein
*The Dead Mother: The Work of André Green* Edited by Gregorio Kohon
*The Fabric of Affect in the Psychoanalytic Discourse* André Green
*The Bi-Personal Field: Experiences of Child Analysis* Antonino Ferro
*The Dove that Returns, the Dove that Vanishes: Paradox and Creativity in Psychoanalysis* Michael Parsons
*Ordinary People, Extra-ordinary Protections: A Post-Kleinian Approach to the Treatment of Primitive Mental States* Judith Mitrani
*The Violence of Interpretation: From Pictogram to Statement* Piera Aulagnier
*The Importance of Fathers: A Psychoanalytic Re-Evaluation* Judith Trowell and Alicia Etchegoyen
*Dreams That Turn Over a Page: Paradoxical Dreams in Psychoanalysis* Jean-Michel Quinodoz
*The Couch and the Silver Screen: Psychoanalytic Reflections on European Cinema* Edited and introduced by Andrea Sabbadini
*In Pursuit of Psychic Change: The Betty Joseph Workshop* Edited by Edith Hargreaves and Arturo Varchevker
*The Quiet Revolution in American Psychoanalysis: Selected Papers of Arnold M. Cooper* Arnold M. Cooper. Edited and introduced by Elizabeth L. Auchincloss
*Seeds of Illness and Seeds of Recovery: The Genesis of Suffering and the Role of Psychoanalysis* Antonino Ferro
*The Work of Psychic Figurability: Mental States Without Representation* César Botella and Sára Botella
*Key Ideas for a Contemporary Psychoanalysis: Misrecognition and Recognition of the Unconscious* André Green
*The Telescoping of Generations: Listening to the Narcissistic Links Between Generations* Haydée Faimberg

*Glacial Times: A Journey Through the World of Madness* Salomon Resnik
*This Art of Psychoanalysis: Dreaming Undreamt Dreams and Interrupted Cries* Thomas H. Ogden
*Psychoanalysis as Therapy and Storytelling* Antonino Ferro
*Psychoanalysis and Religion in the 21st Century: Competitors or Collaborators?* Edited by David M. Black
*Recovery of the Lost Good Object* Eric Brenman
*The Many Voices of Psychoanalysis* Roger Kennedy
*Feeling the Words: Neuropsychoanalytic Understanding of Memory and the Unconscious* Mauro Mancia
*Projected Shadows: Psychoanalytic Reflections on the Representation of Loss in European Cinema* Edited by Andrea Sabbadini
*Encounters with Melanie Klein: Selected Papers of Elizabeth Spillius* Elizabeth Spillius. Edited by Priscilla Roth and Richard Rusbridger
*Constructions and the Analytic Field: History, Scenes and Destiny* Domenico Chianese
*Yesterday, Today and Tomorrow* Hanna Segal
*Psychoanalysis Comparable and Incomparable: The Evolution of a Method to Describe and Compare Psychoanalytic Approaches* David Tuckett *et al.*
*Time, Space and Phantasy* Rosine Jozef Perelberg
*Mind Works: Technique and Creativity in Psychoanalysis* Antonino Ferro
*Rediscovering Psychoanalysis: Thinking and Dreaming, Learning and Forgetting* Thomas H. Ogden

## TITLES IN THE NEW LIBRARY OF PSYCHOANALYSIS TEACHING SERIES

*Reading Freud: A Chronological Exploration of Freud's Writings* Jean-Michel Quinodoz

THE NEW LIBRARY OF PSYCHOANALYSIS

General Editor: Dana Birksted-Breen

# Rediscovering Psychoanalysis

## Thinking and Dreaming, Learning and Forgetting

Thomas H. Ogden

LONDON AND NEW YORK

First published 2009
by Routledge
27 Church Road, Hove, East Sussex BN3 2FA

Simultaneously published in the USA and Canada
by Routledge
270 Madison Avenue, New York, NY 10016

Reprinted 2009

*Routledge is an imprint of the Taylor & Francis Group, an Informa business*



Typeset in Bembo by RefineCatch Limited, Bungay, Suffolk
Printed and bound in Great Britain by TJ International Ltd, Padstow, Cornwall
Paperback cover design by Sandra Heath



This publication has been produced with paper manufactured to strict environmental standards and with pulp derived from sustainable forests.

*British Library Cataloguing in Publication Data*
A catalogue record for this book is available from the British Library

*Library of Congress Cataloging-in-Publication Data*
Ogden, Thomas H.
Rediscovering psychoanalysis : thinking and dreaming, learning and forgetting /
Thomas H. Ogden.
p. cm.
Includes bibliographical references and index.
ISBN 978-0-415-46862-6 (hbk.) – ISBN 978-0-415-46863-3 (pbk.)
1. Psychoanalysis. 2. Psychotherapist and patient. I. Title.
[DNLM: 1. Psychoanalysis 2. Professional–Patient Relations. 3. Psychoanalytic
Therapy. WM 460 O34ra 2008]
RC504.O34 2008
616.89′17—dc22

2008014935

ISBN 978-0-415-46862-6 (hbk)
ISBN 978-0-415-46863-3 (pbk)

For James Grotstein,
my friend, who taught me to marvel

# Contents

# Acknowledgments

I am grateful to the Institute of Psychoanalysis, London, UK for granting permission to publish the following papers:

Chapter 2 is based on "On talking-as-dreaming," *International Journal of Psychoanalysis*, 88: 575–589, 2007, © Institute of Psychoanalysis, London.

Chapter 3 is based on "On psychoanalytic supervision," *International Journal of Psychoanalysis*, 86: 1265–1280, 2005, © Institute of Psychoanalysis, London.

Chapter 4 is based on "On teaching psychoanalysis," *International Journal of Psychoanalysis*, 87: 1069–1085, 2006, © Institute of Psychoanalysis, London.

Chapter 5 is based on "Elements of analytic style: Bion's clinical seminars," *International Journal of Psychoanalysis*, 88: 1185–1200, 2007, © Institute of Psychoanalysis, London.

Chapter 7 is based on "Reading Loewald: Oedipus reconceived," *International Journal of Psychoanalysis*, 87: 651–666, 2006, © Institute of Psychoanalysis, London.

Chapter 8 is based on "Reading Harold Searles," *International Journal of Psychoanalysis*, 88: 353–369, 2007, © Institute of Psychoanalysis, London.

I would like to express my gratitude to Marta Schneider Brody for her invaluable comments on the manuscripts of each of the chapters in this book. I would also like to thank Patricia Marra for the care and thought that she put into the production phase of this volume. I am also grateful to Tom Richardson for the cover illustration which is made up of a mosaic of photographs of the stone labyrinth on the floor of the Chartres Cathedral.

# 1

# Rediscovering psychoanalysis

From the time I was six or seven years old, I was aware of psychoanalysis as a form of treatment for psychological problems, such as feeling unhappy and frightened all the time; but it was not until I was 16, on reading Freud's (1916–1917) *Introductory Lectures on Psycho-Analysis*, that I first discovered psychoanalysis as a set of ideas concerning how we come to be who we are. In using the term *discovered*, I am borrowing a word from a memorable sentence in that introductory lecture series: "I shall not, however, tell it [psychoanalysis as a therapeutic method] to you but shall insist on your discovering it yourself" (1916–1917, p. 431). How better to be introduced to psychoanalysis than by means of an invitation not to be taught, but to discover?

I have spent a good deal of my life since that initial discovery rediscovering psychoanalysis. In an important sense, a psychoanalytic life cannot be spent in any other way. After all, psychoanalysis, both as a set of ideas and as a therapeutic method, is from beginning to end a process of thinking and rethinking, dreaming and re-dreaming, discovering and rediscovering.

The thread that weaves through every page of this book is the idea that it is the analyst's task to engage in a process of rediscovering psychoanalysis in everything that he or she does: in each analytic session, in each supervisory hour, in each meeting of a psychoanalytic seminar, in each reading of an analytic work, and so on.

Rediscovering psychoanalysis entails an act of freedom of thought and an act of humility; an act of renewal and an act of fresh discovery; an act of thinking for oneself and an act of recognition that

> no one who attempts to put forward to-day his views on hysteria and its psychical basis [or any other aspect of psychoanalysis] can

> avoid repeating a great quantity of other people's thoughts . . . Originality is claimed for very little of what will be found in the following pages.
>
> (Breuer and Freud, 1893–1895, pp. 185–186)

In this book, I will discuss three overlapping and interwoven forms of my own experience of rediscovering psychoanalysis: (1) creating psychoanalysis freshly in the process of talking with each patient in each analytic session; (2) rediscovering psychoanalysis in the experience of supervising and teaching psychoanalysis; and (3) "dreaming up" psychoanalysis for oneself in the act of reading and writing about analytic texts and literary works. Although I discuss each of these forms of rediscovery as separate subjects, the topics refuse to keep an orderly queue: thoughts on supervision creep into discussions of talking with patients; close readings of analytic texts invite themselves into discussions of supervision and teaching; responses to creative literature show up in analytic case discussions; and so on. In fact, all three of these forms of rediscovering psychoanalysis are in conversation with one another in each section of this chapter and in each of the succeeding chapters of this book.

## Rediscovering psychoanalysis in the experience of talking with patients

A principal medium, perhaps *the* principal medium, in which I have the opportunity and the responsibility to engage in the work of rediscovering psychoanalysis (and, in so doing, rediscovering what it is to be a psychoanalyst) is the work of being with and talking with patients. Specifically, I view it as my role to create psychoanalysis freshly with each patient in each session of the analysis. A critically important aspect of this rediscovery of psychoanalysis is the creation of ways of talking with each patient that are unique to *that* patient in *that* moment of the analysis. When I speak of talking differently with each patient, I am referring not simply to the unselfconscious use of different tones of voice, rhythms of speech, choice of words, types of formality and informality, and so on, but also to particular ways of being with, and communicating with, another person that could exist between no other two people on this planet.

There are occasions when I am more aware than usual that the patient and I are talking in a way that I talk with no other person in my life. At these moments I have a strong feeling that I am a fortunate man to be able to spend so much of my life inventing with another person ways of talking about what is most important to the patient and to me. In this experience, I am being drawn upon, and am drawing upon myself, emotionally and intellectually, in ways that do not occur in any other part of my life. In this regard, Searles has put into words what I have often felt and thought but have not often had the courage to say, much less write. In discussing an experience that occurred in the psychotherapy of a schizophrenic patient, Searles (1959) states (in a way that only he could have put it), "While we were sitting in silence and a radio not far away was playing a tenderly romantic song . . . I suddenly felt that this man [the patient] was dearer to me than anyone else in the world, including my wife" (p. 294). (See Chapter 8 for a discussion of this and other aspects of Searles's contribution to psychoanalysis.)

It requires a very long time – in my experience, something on the order of a decade or two of full-time clinical practice – to mature as an analyst to a point where one is able, with some consistency, to talk with each of one's patients in a way that is uniquely one's own, and unique to that moment in the analytic conversation with that particular patient. One must have thoroughly learned psychoanalytic technique before one is in a position to "forget it" – that is, to rediscover it for oneself. Talking with patients in the way I am describing requires that the analyst pay very careful attention to the analytic frame. When I am able to speak with a patient in this way, it feels to me that I have ceased "making interpretations" and offering other forms of "analytic interventions," and am instead "simply talking" with the patient. "Simply talking" to a patient, in my experience, usually involves "talking simply" – that is, talking in a simple, clear way that is free of cliché, jargon, and "therapeutic" and other "knowing" tones of voice.

A recent experience in supervision comes to mind in this regard. A seasoned analyst consulted me regarding an analysis that he felt had "ground to a halt." He told me about the various types of interpretations that he had made, none of which seemed to be of any value to the patient. As he spoke, I found myself feeling curious about the analyst. He seemed like an "odd duck" in an interesting and appealing way. Where had he grown up? Probably in the South – maybe Tennessee. What sort of boy had he been? Maybe a little lost, doing the right thing, but with a rebellious streak that he kept a well-guarded secret.

I said to the analyst that it seemed to me that the only thing he had not tried was talking to the patient. I suggested that he stop interpreting and, instead, try simply to talk with the patient as a person who had come to him with the hope and the fear of talking about what was most disturbing in her life. He responded by saying, "You mean I should stop doing analysis with this patient?" I responded by saying, "Yes, if 'doing analysis' means speaking and listening as the analyst you already know how to be. Why don't you see what it would feel like to be an analyst with the patient who is different from the analyst you've been for any other patient you've ever worked with?"

At the end of the consultation session, the analyst said that he felt at a loss to know how to proceed with his patient. I thought that this response to the consultation was a good indication that the analyst had made use of our conversation. When we next met six weeks later, the analyst told me that after our consultation, he felt so lost that during the sessions with his patient that took place in the weeks immediately following the one he had read to me, he found himself saying very little. "Instead, I tried to listen for what I've been missing. Being quiet helped clear my mind, but straining to listen in that way, session after session, was exhausting. I found myself dreading the patient's sessions." The analyst then told me that at the beginning of a session about a month after our consultation, he finally "gave up" and asked the patient, "How can I be of help to you today?" He said that the patient seemed surprised by his question and responded by saying, "I'm so glad you asked me that. I've been feeling like such a failure at psychoanalysis that I've been thinking for a long time that I shouldn't waste your time. I just don't know how to think and talk the way you do. I was afraid before coming here today that you would tell me that you would be ending the analysis." The patient was silent for a couple of minutes and then said, "If you really meant what you said, what I'd like your help with is how to be a better mother to my children. I've been a dreadful mother."

The analyst then told me that for the first time in a very long time he had found what the patient was saying in that session to be genuinely interesting. I was reminded of my own curiosity and imaginings about the analyst in the first consultation session. It seemed to me in retrospect that I was "dreaming up" the analyst in response to his difficulty in "dreaming himself up" as an analyst in his own terms. The analyst responded to his patient by saying, "I think that you are full of dread when you try to be a mother and that makes you feel like a dreadful mother. I think that you find that *trying* to be a mother is not at all the same as simply *being* a mother. I think it terrifies you to feel that you have no idea how to go about just being a mother in a way that feels natural to you."

I said to the analyst that there was no doubt in my mind that he and the patient had begun to talk with one another in a way that they had never before talked with one another, and that it seemed possible to me that neither of them had ever in their lives talked with anyone else in quite that way.

In the sequence described, it was necessary for the analyst to rediscover for himself the experience of becoming an analyst by "giving up" on being the analyst he already knew how to be. In so doing, the analyst began to be able to make room in himself for the experience of being at a loss to know how to be an analyst – how to listen to and how to talk with the patient. The patient was clearly relieved by her conscious and unconscious perception that the analyst had become better able to think and talk for himself and to live with the experience of being a "dreadful analyst" who had no idea what he was doing. It was only at that point that the patient was able to recognize and talk about her feeling of being a dreadful mother. Of course, what I have quoted is not taken from a transcript of what the patient and the analyst said; rather, it is my construction of the analyst's construction of what occurred in the session. This is not a deficiency inherent in the method of enquiry I am using; it is an important element of that method in that it helps capture something of what was true to what occurred at an unconscious level in the analysis, in the supervision, and in the relationship between the analytic experience and the supervisory experience. (In Chapter 3, I discuss this and other aspects of the analytic supervisory experience.)

In discussing this supervisory experience, I have used the term *dreaming* in the phrase '"dreaming up" the analyst.' The conception of dreaming that underlies the idea of dreaming up another person or dreaming oneself into being plays a fundamental role in all that follows in this book. In the tradition of Bion (1962a), I use the term *dreaming* to refer to unconscious psychological work that one does with one's emotional experience. This work of dreaming is achieved by means of a conversation between different aspects of the personality (for example, Freud's [1900] unconscious and preconscious mind,

Bion's [1957] psychotic and non-psychotic parts of the personality, Grotstein's [2000] "dreamer who dreams the dream" and the "dreamer who understands a dream," and Sandler's [1976] "dream-work" and "understanding work"). When an individual's emotional experience is so disturbing that he is unable to dream it (i.e. to do unconscious psychological work with it), he requires the help of another person to dream his formerly undreamable experience. Under these circumstances, it requires two people to think. In the analytic setting, the other person is the analyst; in supervision, it is the supervisor; and in a seminar setting, it is the group leader and the work group mentality (Bion, 1959).

Dreaming occurs continually both during sleep and in waking life, although we have little awareness of our dreaming while we are awake. Reverie (Bion, 1962a; see also Ogden, 1997a,b) and free association constitute forms of preconscious waking dreaming. Dreaming conceived of in this way is not a process of making the unconscious conscious (i.e. making derivatives of the unconscious available to conscious secondary process thinking); rather, it is a process of making the conscious unconscious (i.e. making conscious lived experience available to the richer thought processes involved in unconscious psychological work) (Bion, 1962a). Dreaming is the process by which we attribute personal symbolic meaning to our lived experience, and, in this sense, we dream ourselves and other people into existence. By extension, when an analyst helps a patient or a supervisee to dream his formerly undreamable experience, he is assisting the patient or supervisee in dreaming himself into existence (as an individual or as an analyst).

With this conception of dreaming in mind, I will turn to a form of rediscovery of psychoanalysis that occurred in the course of my work with patients who have very little, if any, capacity for waking dreaming (for example, free association) in the analytic setting. After years of analytic work with a number of such patients, I have found myself (without conscious intention) engaging in seemingly "unanalytic" conversations with these analysands about books, plays, art exhibits, politics, and so on. It took me some time to realize that many of these conversations constituted a form of waking dreaming which I came to think of as "talking-as-dreaming." These conversations tended to be loosely structured, marked by mixtures of primary and secondary process thinking and replete with apparent non sequiturs. "Talking-as-dreaming" superficially appears to be unanalytic; but, to my mind, in the analyses to which I am referring, it represented a significant achievement in that it was often the first form of conversation to take place in these analyses that felt real and alive to both the patient and me.

As time went on in the work with these patients, talking-as-dreaming became established as a natural part of the give-and-take of the analytic relationship and began to move unobtrusively into and out of "talking about dreaming" – that is, self-reflective talk about what was occurring in the analytic relationship and in other parts of the patient's life (past and present). These patients experienced their enhanced capacity to dream and to think and talk about their dreaming as an experience of "waking up" to themselves. Once able to "wake up," their relationship to their waking and sleeping dreaming was profoundly altered – they could begin to think about their dreams as expressions of personal symbolic meaning. In our "discovery" of talking-as-dreaming, these patients and I were rediscovering dreaming and free association.

## Dreaming up psychoanalysis in analytic supervision and teaching

Analytic supervision and the teaching of psychoanalysis in a seminar setting have been, for me, important forms of analytic work in which rediscovery of psychoanalysis takes place. I view not only the clinical practice of psychoanalysis but also analytic supervision and teaching as forms of "guided dream[ing]" (Borges, 1970a, p. 13). In analytic supervision and in case presentations that take place in the seminar setting, it is the task of the supervisory pair and the seminar group to "dream up" the patient whose analysis is being discussed. The patient being presented is not the person who lies down on the couch in the analyst's consulting room. Rather, the patient is a fiction, a character in a story that the supervisee or presenter is creating (dreaming up) in the process of presenting the case. The creation of a fiction is not to be confused with lying. In fact, the two, in the sense I am using the terms, are opposites. Since the analyst cannot bring the patient to the supervisory meeting or to the seminar, he must create in words a fiction that conveys the emotional truth of the experience that he is living with his patient.

From this perspective, the presenter consciously and unconsciously not only *tells*, but also *shows*, the supervisor (or seminar group) the limits of his capacity to dream (to do conscious and unconscious psychological work with) what is occurring in the analysis. The function of the supervisor and the seminar group is that of helping the analyst to dream aspects of the experience with the patient that the analyst has been unable to dream.

Regardless of how many times I take part in the experience of dreaming with a patient, a supervisee, or a presenter, I am each time taken by surprise by the psychological event, and each time find that I have rediscovered the concept of projective identification. Projective identification at its core is a conception of one person participating in thinking/dreaming what another person has been unable to think/dream on his own. I have spent the past thirty-five years rediscovering this concept.

I will close this section by briefly mentioning two areas of ongoing discovery and rediscovery that take place in the context of my experience as an analytic supervisor and teacher of psychoanalysis. The first of these rediscoveries, to which I alluded earlier in this chapter, involves my recognizing that the role of the supervisor and seminar leader is that of assisting the supervisee or seminar member to overcome what he has learned about psychoanalysis in order genuinely to begin the process of becoming a psychoanalyst in his own terms.

The second of these ongoing rediscoveries is my recognizing how critical to my method of teaching psychoanalysis is my practice of reading aloud, line by line, sentence by sentence, the entirety of the analytic or literary text being studied (being read closely). In the next section of this chapter, I will demonstrate what I mean by a close reading of a piece of writing. I have found that reading texts aloud in this way allows the seminar members and me to hear and feel the ways in which the sound of the words, the voice of the speaker, the author's word choice, the rhythm and structure of the sentences, and so on, together create emotional effects that are inseparable from the content of what is being said. In hearing the sentences read aloud, it becomes clear that words are not merely carrying cases for ideas. Rather, words – whether it be the words of an analytic text, a poem, a short story, a patient's comment to the analyst in the waiting room, or the analyst's response to a patient's dream – do not simply re-present the writer's/speaker's experience, they create an experience for the first time in the very act of being read/spoken/heard.

## Analytic reading and writing as forms of "dreaming up" psychoanalysis

Writing about analytic works, poetry, and other imaginative literature has been critical to my development as an analyst, and has served as an important medium in which I continue to rediscover psychoanalysis. In this book, I offer close readings of analytic papers by Loewald and Searles; transcripts of clinical seminars conducted by Bion; a passage from a short story by Lydia Davis; some comments on novels by DeLillo and Coetzee; and a monologue from the film *Raising Arizona*. In these discussions, I am not simply explicating the work of Loewald, Searles, Bion, and others. I am "dreaming up" the works for myself and then inviting the reader to do the same, both with the text about which I am writing and with my "dreamt-up" version of that text. When I speak of "dreaming up" a text, I am referring to the conscious and unconscious psychological work of making something of one's own with the text one is reading. In this process, the text is the starting point for the reader's own creative act that is unique to him and reflects his own "peculiar mentality" (Bion, 1987, p. 224).

When I begin to write about an analytic text, I have only a vague sense of what I think about the aspect of psychoanalysis that the text addresses. I write to find out what I think. I aspire in my writing about analytic texts to do with the text something that is, in some small measure, akin to what Glenn Gould (1974) said that he tried to do with each piece of music he played: "I recreate the work. I turn performance into composition." Similarly, in writing about an analytic text (for example, individual works of Bion, Loewald, and Searles in Chapters 5, 7, and 8, respectively) or an analyst's life-work (Bion's theory of thinking in Chapter 6), I try to turn close critical reading and writing into composition, I attempt to turn the author's discovery into a discovery of my own. My discovery, my act of dreaming up the text, is different from, and sometimes at odds with, the discovery/dream that the author is making.

Let me elaborate here on the way I am using the term *dreaming*. In waking life, our conscious thinking is, to a very large extent, limited by sequential, cause-and-effect, secondary process logic. In our dream-life, we are able to engage in a far more profound type of thinking. In dreaming, one is "able to imagine with a freedom . . . [one] does not have in waking" (Borges, 1980, p. 34). We are able, while dreaming, to view a situation from many points of view (and points in time) simultaneously. A single figure or situation in a dream may encompass a lifetime of experiences – both real and imagined – with one or with many people. The dreamer has the opportunity to rework the situation – to try it this way and that way, to view it from this perspective and that perspective, separately and together. The dreamer brings to bear upon his rendering of an emotional situation in a dream the most primitive and the most mature aspects of himself, and, most importantly, these aspects of the self talk to one another in a mutually transformative way.

What we dream when we are asleep is a rediscovery of our waking experience, a rediscovery that not only sheds light on that lived experience, but transforms it into something new, something with which we can do unconscious psychological work. That psychological work (the work of dreaming) is work that we have not been able to achieve in the more limited medium of waking thinking.

This broadened conception of dreaming will serve as a framework for a greater understanding of what I mean by dreaming a text in the act of reading it and writing about it. In writing about Loewald's (1979) "The Waning of the Oedipus Complex" (Chapter 7), I am not only concerned with what Loewald thought, I am interested in what I can do with what Loewald wrote. It might be said that Loewald had a dream-thought, and that his act of writing his paper was his dreaming that thought. Once dreamt/written, Loewald's dream/paper becomes a "dream-thought" that I have the opportunity to dream in the act of reading it and writing about it. It is only to the extent that I am able to dream ("recreate") Loewald's paper as *my* dream that there is any reason for a reader to read my work, and not simply read Loewald's and leave it at that.

In talking about dreaming an analytic text, I am reminded of Borges's comment, "Dreams . . . ask us something, and we don't know how to answer, they give us the answer, and we are astonished" (Borges, 1980, p. 35). The "answer" that we get from dreaming in the act of critical reading and writing is not the solution to a puzzle; it is the beginning of a creative act in its own right. Moreover, in saying, "Dreams ask us something," Borges, I believe, is suggesting that dreams ask something of us. For example, an analytic text, when viewed as a dream-thought, is a thought asking to be dreamt by the critical reader or writer. When the dream-thought is an analytic text, the "answer" (more accurately, the response) is psychoanalysis rediscovered in the reader's or the critical writer's own terms.

To illustrate what I mean when I say that reading and writing are forms of dreaming, I will briefly discuss a couple of sentences taken from the end of a short story by Lydia Davis (2007), "What You Learn About the Baby":

> How responsible he is, to the limits of his capacity . . . How he is curious, to the limits of his understanding; how he attempts to approach what arouses his curiosity, to the limits of his motion; how confident he is, to the limits of his knowledge; how masterful he is, to the limits of his competence; how he derives satisfaction from another face before him, to the limits of his attention; how he asserts his needs, to the limits of his force.
>
> (Davis, 2007, p. 124)

The title of the story, "What You Learn About the Baby," frames everything that follows, including the final lines just cited. It is a remarkable title, not for what it says, but for what it withholds. Virtually every word of the six-word title contributes to its somewhat eerie emotional restraint: What [could there be a less descriptive word?] you [a surprisingly impersonal pronoun that takes the place of "I"] learn about [not "learn from" or "learn with," much less "get to know"] the [not the possessive pronouns "my" or "your," but the chillingly impersonal article, "the"] baby.

Despite the chill created by this use of language, these final sentences of the story are quite beautiful. The repetition (seven times) of clauses or sentences that begin with the word *how*, and are divided in the middle by a comma, creates a sound and rhythm suggestive of a lullaby. But this is no ordinary lullaby. Words are meticulously being refined, for example, as the word *responsible* is qualified by the phrase *to the limits of his capacity*, and the word *curious* is carefully pruned by the phrase *to the limits of his understanding*.

And this is no ordinary mother. (The reader is never told whether the speaker is a mother or whether the speaker is a man or a woman. I will indicate with a question mark where I am making a conjecture about something left in doubt in the story.) The speaker (mother?), with her (?) highly crafted use of language, is at once tightly holding the baby, and holding him at arm's length; at once tender, perspicaciously observant, and emotionally distant; at once devoted to the baby, and perhaps even more devoted to writing "about the baby."

What is being raised in this passage, and in the story as a whole, is the never spoken question, "Is the speaker a mother-who-is-a-writer or a writer-who-is-a-mother?" No doubt the answer is both, but that does not solve the emotional problem created in the writing: How is the speaker to be both completely a writer (which, to my ear, is no doubt the case) and completely a mother (about which there is some doubt)?

The speaker succeeds in finding at least a partial solution to this emotional problem by accepting her strangeness as a mother – what kind of mother allows herself to talk about "the baby" (instead of "my baby") or parses words with such subtlety in describing her (?) baby? The acceptance of her (?) own strangeness (as reflected in the ease and grace with which she writes such oddly motherly things) seems to allow the speaker also to accept the strangeness of her (?) baby – babies are indeed very strange creatures.

The pleasure that this mother (?) takes in her (?) baby includes a profound appreciation of the ironies that saturate his situation in life: "How masterful he is, to the limits of his competence." The words *how masterful* carry the double meaning of a question (how masterful?) and an appreciation (how masterful!). Whether it is a part of a question or an expression of amazement, the word *masterful* bumps awkwardly, humorously into the phrase *to the limits of his competence*. The use of irony here seems to me to convey a sense of the way in which the writerliness of the mother (?) provides a psychological/literary sanctuary into which the speaker may go when she needs a rest from her (?) baby, a place the infant cannot conceive of, a place into which he is not invited.

The sequence of clauses culminates in what, for me, is the most powerful of the observations: "how he asserts his needs, to the limits of his force." The word *force* (the final word of the story) is a surprising word – darkly ominous. The word stands in stark contrast with the six words that have stood in a similar place in the six previous clauses: "capacity," "understanding," "motion," "knowledge," "competence," "attention." The word *force* breaks the rules of constraint that have held sway up to this point: all bets are off, no previous "understandings" between mother (?) and infant (or between writer and reader) hold. The baby will use every means available to him to get what he needs. There will be no compromises; there will be no sanctuaries in which to find respite from the baby.

The subtle mixture of feelings and complexity of voice in this passage defies paraphrase. Responding to this passage, in the act of writing/dreaming it, is, for me, an experience of rediscovering "primary maternal preoccupation" (Winnicott, 1956), the mother's healthy hatred of her baby, the analyst's healthy hatred of his patient (Winnicott, 1947); it is also an experience in psychoanalytic "ear training" (Pritchard, 1994); and, perhaps most of all, it is an experience of emotionally responding to, and making something of my own with, the extraordinary beauty and power of language artfully used.

I will now leave it to the reader to dream this book, to dream my dream-thought, to make something of his or her own in the experience of reading.

# 2

# On talking-as-dreaming

> 'Auntie, speak to me! I'm frightened because it's so dark.' His aunt answered him: 'What good would that do? You can't see me.' 'That doesn't matter,' replied the child, 'if anyone speaks, it gets light.'
>
> (Freud, 1905, p. 224, n.1)

I take as fundamental to an understanding of psychoanalysis the idea that the analyst must invent psychoanalysis anew with each patient. This is achieved in no small measure by means of an ongoing experiment, within the terms of the psychoanalytic situation, in which patient and analyst create ways of talking to one another that are unique to each analytic pair at a given moment in the analysis.

In this chapter, I will focus primarily on forms of talking generated by patient and analyst that may at first seem "unanalytic" because the patient and analyst are talking about such things as books, poems, films, rules of grammar, etymology, the speed of light, the taste of chocolate, and so on. Despite appearances, it has been my experience that such "unanalytic" talk often allows a patient and analyst who have been unable to dream together to begin to be able to do so. I will refer to talking of this sort as "talking-as-dreaming." Like free association (and unlike ordinary conversation), talking-as-dreaming tends to include considerable primary process thinking and what appear to be non sequiturs (from the perspective of secondary process thinking).

When an analysis is a "going concern" (Winnicott, 1964, p. 27), the patient and analyst are able to engage both individually and with one another in a process of dreaming. The area of "overlap" of the patient's dreaming and the analyst's dreaming is the place where analysis occurs (Winnicott, 1971, p. 38). The patient's dreaming, under such circumstances, manifests itself in the form of free associations (or, in child analysis, in the form of playing); the analyst's waking-dreaming often takes the form of reverie experience. When a patient is unable to dream, this difficulty becomes the most pressing aspect of the analysis. It is these situations that are the focus of this chapter.

I view dreaming as the most important psychoanalytic function of the mind: where there is unconscious "dream-work," there is also unconscious "understanding-work" (Sandler, 1976, p. 40); where there is an unconscious "dreamer who dreams the dream" (Grotstein, 2000, p. 5), there is also an unconscious "dreamer who understands the dream" (p. 9). If this were not the case, only dreams that are remembered and interpreted in the analytic setting or in self-analysis would accomplish psychological work. Few analysts today would support the idea that only remembered and interpreted dreams facilitate psychological growth.

The analyst's participation in the patient's talking-as-dreaming entails a distinctively analytic way of being with a patient. It is at all times directed by the analytic task of helping the patient to become more fully alive to his experience, more fully human. Moreover, the experience of talking-as-dreaming is different from other conversations that bear a superficial resemblance to it (such as talk that goes nowhere or even a substantive conversation between a husband and wife, a parent and child, or a brother and sister). What makes talking-as-dreaming different is that the analyst engaged in this form of conversation is continually observing and talking with himself about two inextricably interwoven levels of this emotional experience: (1) talking-as-dreaming as an experience of the patient coming into being in the process of dreaming his lived emotional experience; and (2) the analyst and patient thinking about and, at times, talking about the experience of understanding (getting to know) something of the meanings of the emotional situation being faced in the process of dreaming.

In what follows, I will offer two clinical illustrations of talking-as-dreaming. The first involves a patient and analyst talking together in a way that represents a form of dreaming an aspect of the patient's (and, in a sense, her father's) experience that the patient previously had been almost entirely unable to dream. In the second clinical example, patient and analyst engage in a form of talking-as-dreaming in which the analyst participates in the patient's early efforts to "dream himself up," to "dream himself into existence."

## A theoretical context

The theoretical context for the present contribution is grounded in Bion's (1962a, b, 1992) radical transformation of the psychoanalytic conception of dreaming and of not being able to dream. Just as Winnicott shifted the focus of analytic theory and practice from play (as a symbolic representation of the child's internal world) to the experience of playing, Bion shifted the focus from the symbolic content of thoughts to the process of thinking, and from the symbolic meaning of dreams to the process of dreaming.

For Bion (1962a), "alpha-function" (an as-yet-unknown, and perhaps unknowable, set of mental functions) transforms raw "sense impressions related to emotional experience" (p. 17) into "alpha-elements" that can be linked to form affect-laden dream-thoughts. A dream-thought presents an emotional problem with which the individual must struggle (Bion, 1962a, b; Meltzer, 1983), thus supplying the impetus for the development of the capacity for dreaming (which is synonymous with unconscious thinking). "[Dream-]-thoughts require an apparatus to cope with them . . . Thinking [dreaming] has to be called into existence to cope with [dream-]thoughts" (Bion, 1962b, pp. 110–111). In the absence of alpha-function (either one's own or that provided by another person), one cannot dream and therefore cannot make use of (do unconscious psychological work with) one's lived emotional experience, past and present. Consequently, a person unable to dream is trapped in an endless, unchanging world of what is.

Undreamable experience may have its origins in trauma – unbearably painful emotional experience, such as the early death of a parent, the death of a child, military combat, rape or imprisonment in a death camp. But undreamable experience may also arise from "intrapsychic trauma" – that is, experiences of being overwhelmed by conscious and unconscious fantasy. The latter form of trauma may stem from the failure of the mother to adequately hold the infant and contain his primitive anxieties or from a constitutional psychic fragility that renders the individual in infancy and childhood unable to dream his emotional experience, even with the help of a good-enough mother. Undreamable experience – whether it be the consequence of predominantly external or intrapsychic forces – remains with the individual as "undreamt dreams" in such forms as psychosomatic illness, split-off psychosis, "dis-affected" states (McDougall, 1984), pockets of autism (Tustin, 1981), severe perversions (de M'Uzan, 2003), and addictions.

It is this conception of dreaming and of not being able to dream that underlies my own thinking regarding psychoanalysis as a therapeutic process. As I have previously discussed (Ogden, 2004a, 2005a), I view psychoanalysis as an experience in which patient and analyst engage in an experiment within the analytic frame that is designed to create conditions in which the analysand (with the analyst's participation) may be able to dream formerly undreamable emotional experience (his "undreamt dreams"). I view talking-as-dreaming as an improvisation in the form of a loosely structured conversation (concerning virtually any subject) in which the analyst participates in the patient's dreaming previously undreamt dreams. In so doing, the analyst facilitates the patient's dreaming himself more fully into existence.

## Fragments of two analyses

I will now present clinical accounts of analytic work with two patients who were severely limited in their ability to dream their emotional experience in the form of free associations or in other types of dreaming. In both of these analyses, the patient was eventually able, with the analyst's participation, to begin to engage in genuine dreaming in the form of talking-as-dreaming.

### *Talking-as-dreaming formerly undreamt dreams*

Ms L, a highly intelligent and accomplished woman, began analysis because she was tormented by intense fears that her seven-year-old son, Aaron, would fall ill and die. She also suffered from an almost unbearable fear of dying that for periods of weeks at a time had rendered her unable to function. These fears were compounded by her feeling that her husband was so self-centered as to be unable to care for their son if anything were to happen to her. Ms L was so preoccupied with her fears concerning her son's life and her own that she could speak of practically nothing else in the first years of analysis. Other aspects of her life seemed to be of no emotional significance to her. The idea that the patient was coming to see me to think about her life held virtually no meaning – she came to each of her daily sessions with the hope that I would be able to free her of her fears. Ms L's dream-life consisted almost entirely of "dreams" that were not dreams (Bion, 1962a; Ogden, 2003a); that is, she was unchanged by the experience of the repetitive dreams and nightmares in which she was helpless to prevent one catastrophe after another. My own reverie experience was sparse and unusable for purposes of psychological work (see Ogden, 1997a, b for detailed discussions of the analytic use of reverie experience).

From the beginning of the analysis, the patient's way of speaking was distinctive. She spoke spasmodically, blurting out clumps of words, as if trying to get as many words as she could into each breath of air. It seemed to me that Ms L was afraid that at any moment she would lose her breath or would be cut off by my telling her that I had heard enough and could not stand to hear another word.

By the beginning of the second year of analysis, the patient appeared to have lost all hope that I could be of any help to her. She barely paused after I spoke before continuing the line of thought that I had momentarily interrupted. She seemed hardly at all interested in what I had to say – perhaps because she could hear almost immediately in my tone of voice and rhythm of speech that what I was about to say would not contain the relief that she sought. The patient responded to the combination of fear and despair that she was feeling by flooding the sessions with clump after clump of words that had the effect of drowning out (both for herself and me) any opportunity for genuine dreaming and thinking. In a session that took place during this period of the analysis, I said to Ms L that I thought that she felt that there was so little of her that she did not have sufficient substance to achieve change through thinking and talking. (I had in mind her inability to speak without chopping her sentences and paragraphs into bits. The relief that she hoped I would supply was the only means by which she could imagine her life changing.) After I made this observation, the patient paused slightly longer than usual before continuing with what she was saying. I commented that what I had just said must have felt useless to her.

In the months preceding the session that I will present, the patient's speech had become somewhat less pressured. She was able for the first time to talk with feeling about her childhood experience. Up to that point, it was as if the patient felt that there was not "time" (i.e. psychological room) for thinking and talking about anything other than her efforts "to cope," to keep herself from losing her mind. The patient's fear of dying and her worries about Aaron diminished to the point that she was able to read again for the first time since Aaron was born. Reading and the study of literature had been a passion of the patient's in college and in graduate school. Aaron was born only a few months after she completed her doctoral thesis.

The session that I will discuss was a Monday session that the patient began by telling me that over the weekend she had re-read J. M. Coetzee's novel, *Disgrace* (1999). (Ms L and I had briefly spoken about Coetzee's work in the course of the previous year of analysis. Like Ms L, I greatly admire Coetzee as a writer and no doubt this had come through in the brief exchanges we had had about him.) Ms L said, "There is something about that book [which is set in post-apartheid South Africa] that draws me back to it. The narrator [a college professor] tries to bring himself back to life – if he ever was alive – by having sex with one of his students. It seems inevitable that the girl will turn him in, and when she does, he refuses to defend himself. He won't even go through the motions of saying the repentant words to the academic council that his friends and colleagues are urging him to say. And so he gets fired. It is as if he has felt like a disgrace his whole life and that this incident is only the latest evidence of this state, evidence he cannot and will not attempt to refute."

Although the patient was speaking in her characteristic way (blurting out words in clumps), it was unmistakable that a change was occurring: Ms L was speaking with genuine vitality in her voice about something that did not relate directly to her fears about Aaron's safety or her own health. (It must be borne in mind that this change did not arise *de novo* in the session being described. Rather, it developed over the course of years, beginning with a note of humour here, an unintended, but appreciated, pun there, an occasional dream that had a small measure of aliveness, and a reverie of mine that had unexpected vitality. Very slowly such scattered events became elements of an unselfconscious way of being that came alive in the form that I am in the process of describing.)

I did not tell the patient my thought that she, in speaking about the narrator, may also have been speaking to herself and to me about a psychological conflict of her own – that is, that one aspect of herself (identified with the narrator's refusal to lie) seemed to be at odds with another aspect of herself (for whom fears of death crowded out the possibility for genuine thinking, feeling, and talking). To have said any of this to Ms L would have been equivalent to waking the patient from what may have been one of her first experiences of dreaming in the analysis in order to tell her my understanding of the dream. It was nonetheless important that I make this interpretation to myself silently because, as will be seen, I was at the time engaging in something very similar to what Ms L was doing in that I, too, was evading thinking and feeling.

I said to Ms L, "Coetzee's voice in *Disgrace* is one of the most unsentimental voices I have ever read. He makes it clear in every sentence that he deplores rounding the edges of any human experience. An experience is what it is, no more and no less." In saying this, I felt as if I was entering into a form of thinking and talking with the patient that was different from any exchange that had previously occurred in the analysis.

Ms L, somewhat to my surprise, continued the conversation by saying, "There's something about what's happening *between* the characters and *in* the characters – no matter how awful it is – that is oddly right."

I then said something that even at the time felt like a non sequitur: "You can hear in Coetzee's early books a writer who did not yet know who he was as a writer or even as a person. He's awkward, trying this and trying that. I sometimes feel embarrassed with him." (I felt that the words "with him" said more of what I was feeling in the session with Ms L than would have been conveyed by the words "for him." I was putting the emphasis on my own, and what I sensed to be the patient's, feelings of self-consciousness in response to the awkwardness of our efforts at talking/thinking/dreaming in this new way.)

Ms L then said, in another of our apparent non sequiturs, "Even after the rape of the narrator's daughter and the shooting of the dogs that the daughter loved so much, the narrator found ways to hang onto the fragments of his humanity that remained alive for him. After helping the veterinarian euthanize dogs that had no one and no place on this earth to which they belonged, he tried to spare the corpses the indignity of being treated like garbage. He made it his business to be there very early in the morning to put the corpses into the cremation machine himself instead of giving the bodies to the workmen who ran the machine. He couldn't bear to see the workers use shovels to smash the dogs' legs which were stiffened and outstretched with rigor mortis. The outstretched legs made it harder to get the corpses to fit into the door of the machine." There was sadness and warmth in Ms L's voice as she talked. As the patient was speaking, I was reminded of talking with a close friend soon after he had come home from a hospitalization during which it had seemed all but certain that he would die. He told me that he had learned one thing from the experience: "Dying doesn't take courage. It's like being on a conveyor belt taking you to the end." He added, "Dying is easy. You don't have to do anything." I remembered feeling humbled, as he and I talked, by the dignity with which he had faced death in the hospital and by the way he used his capacity for irony and wit, even while emotionally and physically exhausted, to keep from being crushed by the experience.

As I re-focused on Ms L, I responded to what she had been saying about the handling of the dogs' corpses (and the compassionate way in which she had been saying it) by commenting, "The narrator kept making that small gesture [in connection with the cremation of the dogs] even though he knew that what he was doing was so insignificant as to be imperceptible to anybody or anything else in the universe." As I was saying this, I began to think (in a way that was new for me in this analysis) about the effect of the terrible deaths in Ms L's life. The patient had told me early on in the analysis, and then again in a session a few months prior to the one being discussed, that her father's first wife and their three-year-old daughter had been killed in a car accident. (The patient deeply loved her father and felt loved by him.) On the two occasions that Ms L had mentioned the death of her father's first wife and daughter, she did so as if presenting a piece of information that I should know about because analysts (with their stereotypic ways of thinking) tend to make a big deal about such things. I was able at this point to make use of the silent interpretation that I had made earlier to myself regarding the way the patient (and I) were evading thinking/dreaming/speaking/remembering what was true to the emotional experience that was occurring. In my work with Ms L, I had, for more than a year, been unable and perhaps unwilling to think/dream/remember and keep alive in myself the enormous (unimaginable) pain that the patient's father and the patient had experienced in relation to the death of his first wife and their daughter. I was astounded by my inability to have kept alive in me the emotional impact of those deaths.

At that point in the session I was able to begin to dream (to do conscious and unconscious psychological work with) what I now perceived to be the patient's feelings of "disgrace" for being alive "in place of" her father's wife and daughter and in place of the parts of her father that had died with them. Ms L responded to what I said about the narrator's "insignificant," but important, gestures by saying, "In Coetzee's books dying is not the worst thing that can happen to a person. For some reason, I find that idea comforting. I don't know why, but I'm reminded of a line I love from Coetzee's memoir. He says near the end something like: 'All we can do is to persist stupidly, doggedly in our repeated failures.'" Ms L laughed deeply in a way I had never heard her laugh before as she said, "Dogs are everywhere today. I am very fond of dogs. They're the innocents of the animal kingdom." She then became more pensive and said, "There's nothing glamorous about repeated failures while they're happening. I feel like such a failure as a mother. I can't lie to myself and pretend that my obsession with Aaron's dying isn't felt by him and doesn't scare the life out of him. I didn't intend to put it that way – 'scare the life out of him' – but that is what I feel I'm doing to him. I'm terrified that I'm killing him with my fear – that I'm scaring the life out of him, and I can't stop doing it. That's my 'disgrace.'" Ms L cried as she spoke. It seemed clear to me at this moment that Ms L's father's response to his "unthinkable" losses had scared the life out of her.

I said, "I think that you've felt like a disgrace your whole life. Your father's pain was unbearable not only to him, but to you. You couldn't help your father with his unimaginable pain. His pain was such a complicated thing for you – you're still in the grip of it with him – pain beyond what anyone can take in." This was the first time in the analysis that I addressed the patient's inability not only to help her father, but also to dream her experience of her response to his pain. I thought, but did not say, that it felt shameful to her that she felt angry at her father for not having been able to be the father she wished he were. Moreover, she took that anger out on her husband in the form of demeaning him for what she perceived to be his inadequacy as a father to their son.

Ms L did not respond directly to what I said, and instead said, "I think that it's odd that I think of the characters in Coetzee's book as courageous. They don't think of themselves that way. But they do feel that way to me. In *Life & Times of Michael K* [Coetzee, 1983], Michael K [a black man in apartheid South Africa] builds a cart out of scraps of wood and metal. He wheels his dying mother toward the town where she was born so she can die there – it is the closest thing to a home that she has ever had. I don't think Michael K felt courageous as he was doing it. He just knew that that was what he had to do. It was a doomed effort. I think he knew that from the beginning – I think I did, too. But it had to be done. It was the right thing to do. I like the fact that Coetzee's narrators are often women. In *The Age of Iron* [Coetzee, 1990], the woman narrator [a white woman living in apartheid South Africa] took in the homeless black man and felt guilty and pitied him and grew to admire him and became angry with him and even loved him in her own odd way. She never once pulled a punch in the way she talked to herself and to him. You and I can sometimes be like that. We've done some of that today – not entirely, but enough so I feel stronger now, which is not to say happier. But being stronger is what I need more than feeling happier." I could hear in the sound of Ms L's voice that she felt, but could not yet say (even to herself), that she felt admiration and anger and her own odd brand of love for me and that she hoped that I, one day, might feel all of this for her.

The actual course of the session had a far more meandering quality than the account I have been able to give. The patient and I drifted from topic to topic, book to book, feeling to feeling, without experiencing the need to tie one to the next, or to think in a logical way, or to respond directly to what the other had said. We spoke of Coetzee's choice to live in Adelaide, Australia, John Berger's scathingly anti-capitalist Booker Prize acceptance speech, our disappointment in Coetzee's two most recent novels, and so on. It is impossible for me to say which of these subjects were spoken about in the session under discussion and which were spoken about in subsequent sessions. Neither can I say with any certainty which parts of the dialogue that I have presented from the session were spoken by Ms L and which parts by me.

As the emotional experience of this session evolved in subsequent weeks and months, the patient told me that her father had had bouts of severe depression as she was growing up and that she had felt responsible for helping him to recover from them. She said that she had often sat with him for long periods of time as "he sobbed uncontrollably, choking on his tears." As Ms L described these experiences with her father, it occurred to me that her talking in clumps of words, cramming as many words as she could into a breath of air, may have been related to her experience of her father choking on his tears while sobbing uncontrollably. Perhaps, unable to dream her experience with her father, she had somatized her undreamt dreams (and his) in her pattern of speaking and breathing.

In sum, in the session I have discussed, the way Ms L and I talked about books served as a form of talking-as-dreaming. It was an experience in dreaming that was neither exclusively the patient's dream nor mine. Ms L had only rarely been able to achieve a state of waking-dreaming to that point in the analysis. Consequently, she had been trapped in a timeless world of split-off undreamable experience that she feared had not only robbed her father and herself of a good deal of their lives, but also was killing her child. Ms L had developed psychosomatic symptoms (her manner of speech and breathing) and intense fears of death at the psychological point at which she was no longer able to dream *her* experience of her father's depression or her anger at him. As the session under discussion progressed, the patient was able to dream (in the form of talking-as-dreaming) formerly undreamable experience of and with her father. This talking-as-dreaming moved unobtrusively into and out of talking about dreaming. I view such movement between talking-as-dreaming and talking-about-dreaming as a hallmark of psychoanalysis when it is "a going concern."

## *Talking-as-dreaming oneself into existence*

I shall now describe a clinical experience in which talking-as-dreaming served as a primary means through which a patient was able to begin to develop his own rudimentary capacity "to dream himself into being."

Mr B grew up under circumstances of extreme neglect. He was the youngest of five children born to an Irish Catholic family living in a working-class suburb of Boston. The patient, as a child, was tormented by his three older brothers who humiliated and frightened him at every opportunity. Mr B did what he could to "become invisible." He would spend as little time as possible at home and, while at home, would draw as little attention to himself as he could. He learned early on that bringing his problems to his parents' attention only made matters worse in that it would lead to his brothers' redoubling their brutalizing of him. Nonetheless, he tenaciously clung to the hope that his parents, particularly his mother, would see what was happening without his having to tell them.

Beginning at age seven or eight, Mr B immersed himself in reading.

He would literally read shelf after shelf of books at the public library. He told me that I should not mistake reading with either intelligence or the acquisition of knowledge: "My reading was pure escapism. I lost myself in the stories, and, a week after reading a book, I couldn't tell you a thing about it." (In a previous contribution [Ogden, 1989a], I have discussed the use of reading as a sensation-dominated experience that may serve as an autistic defense.)

Despite the fact that I liked Mr B, I found the first four years of the analysis to be rather lifeless. Mr B spoke slowly, deliberately, as if considering every word that he said before saying it. Over time, he and I came to view this as a reflection of his fear that I would either use what he said as a way of humiliating him (in the fraternal transference) or somehow fail to recognize what was most important, and yet unstated, in what he said (in the maternal transference).

It was not until the fifth year of this five-session-per-week analysis that the patient began to be able to remember and tell me his dreams. Among these early dreams was one in which there was a single horrifying image of a shabby wax figure of a Madonna and infant in a wax museum. What was most disturbing about the image was the vacant stare that each was giving the other.

The session that I will describe occurred shortly after the Madonna-and-infant dream. It was a period of analysis in which the patient and I were beginning to be able to talk to one another in a way that held some vitality, and yet this way of talking was still so new as to feel brittle and, at times, a bit awkward.

Mr B began the session by saying that at work he had overheard a woman saying to a colleague that she could not bear to watch the Coen brothers' film *Raising Arizona* because she could not see the humor in the kidnapping of a baby.[1] Mr B then asked me, "Have you seen that movie?" This was only the second or third time in the entire analysis that Mr B had asked me a direct question of this sort. The analytic relationship to that point was one in which the focus was almost entirely on the patient's experience and state of mind, with virtually no explicit allusion to – much less questioning or discussing – my experience. It did not feel entirely natural to simply answer his question, but I

[1] In *Raising Arizona*, a couple (played by Nicolas Cage and Holly Hunter), unable to conceive a baby of their own, steal one of the quintuplets recently born to Nathan Arizona and his wife. Cage and Hunter convince themselves that a family with so many babies would hardly notice that one of them was missing.

could not imagine responding by reflexively returning the question to the patient by, for instance, asking why he had asked the question or suggesting that he had been afraid that I would not understand the significance of what he was about to say. I told Mr B that I had seen the film a number of times. I was aware only as I was saying these words that in responding in this way I was saying to the patient more than he had asked of me. I experienced this not as a slip but as a line that I was adding to a squiggle game. Nonetheless, I was a bit worried that what I had added would be experienced by the patient as intrusive and would precipitate the equivalent of a play disruption.

Mr B moved his head on the pillow of the analytic couch in a way that conveyed a sense of surprise that I had responded as I had. It seemed clear to both of us that we were in uncharted waters. As this emotional shift was occurring, I had in mind a number of thoughts about the transference-countertransference. Mr B, in asking me a direct question, had dared to make himself less "invisible," and I had, without conscious intention, responded in kind. Moreover, he was inviting me to join him in talking about the work of two brothers, the Coen brothers, who made extraordinary things together. Making something (becoming someone) with one's brother was an experience that the patient had missed out on with his own brothers. Perhaps his introducing the Coen brothers into the analysis reflected a wish to have such an experience with me. I decided not to say any of this to the patient because I believed that it would have distracted from and undermined the tentative movement toward emotional intimacy that the patient and I were making.

With an intensity of feeling in his voice that was unusual for him, Mr B said that he thought that the woman whom he had overheard talking about *Raising Arizona* was treating the film as if it were a documentary: "It seems crazy for me to get worked up about this, but that film is one of my favorites. I have seen it so many times that I know the dialogue by heart, so I hate to hear the film disparaged in a mindless way."[2]

I said, "There's irony in every frame of that film. Sometimes irony can be frightening. You never know when it'll be turned on you." (Even though the patient had unconsciously commented on what

[2] I am again and again impressed by the way in which film images and narratives seem to share some of the evocative power of dream images and narratives (see Gabbard, 1997a, b; Gabbard and Gabbard, 1999).

was going on between us – our being less mindless and rigid with one another than had been our pattern – it seemed to me that to have responded at that level would have disrupted what I sensed was becoming talking-as-dreaming.)

Mr B said, "The movie is not a documentary, it's a dream. It opens with Nicolas Cage being photographed for mug shots after being arrested for one bungled petty crime after the next. It's as if right from the start two levels of reality are being introduced: the person and the photograph. I've never thought of the opening of the film in that way before. And the huge guy on the motorcycle – more an archetype than a person – lives in the film in a parallel reality that is disconnected from the reality of the other parts of the film. I'm sorry for getting so carried away." The patient's voice was full of the excitement of a child.

I asked, "Why not get carried away?" (This was not a rhetorical question. I was saying in a highly condensed way that there had been very good reasons for the patient as a child to feel that it was dangerous to talk with excitement in his voice, but that those reasons were true to another reality, the reality of the past, which for him often eclipsed the reality of the present.)

Mr B went on without a pause to say, "My favorite part of the film is the voice-over at the end [which takes place after Nicolas Cage and Holly Hunter have returned the baby that they took and Holly Hunter has told Nicolas Cage that she is leaving him]. As he lies awake in bed next to her, he speaks in a way that is somewhere between thinking while falling asleep and dreaming. In his voice, there is a feeling that he'd do anything to have a second chance to get it right, but he knows himself well enough to realize that odds are he'll screw it up again. Now that I think of it, the end is a repetition, in a much richer form, of the opening scene in which the mug shots are being taken after each of his arrests. He can never get it right. But by the end, you know him and it hurts to see him never getting it right. He has a good heart. In the voice-over monologue at the end, he imagines the life of the baby, Nathan, Jr. [the baby they took and then returned to his family]. Cage can make out vaguely in the future his own invisible presence in the life of the child as he grows up. The child can feel someone lovingly watching him, feeling proud of him, but the child can't quite connect the feeling with a particular person." (Of course, I heard this as the patient's unconscious way of telling me that he felt lovingly watched over by me. In addition, the beloved baby that Mr B and I were dreaming/conceiving seemed to "embody" the analytic experience itself that, in this session, was being freshly "brought to life" in the process of the patient and me dreaming together.)

I said to Mr B, "In the last scene Nicolas Cage also imagines a couple – maybe it's himself and Holly Hunter – with their own children and grandchildren."

Mr B excitedly interrupted me to say, "Yes, his dream at the end has it both ways. I want to believe he's looking into the future. No, it's a softer feeling than that. It is a feeling of *maybe*. Even for such a screw-up as Cage, if he can imagine something, it might happen. No, that sounds so trite. I can't find the right way of putting it. It's so frustrating. If he can dream it, it has happened in the dream. No, I can't say it the way I mean it."

I chose not to focus directly on the meaning of the patient's difficulty in finding the right words – which may have derived from his anxiety about the love that he was feeling for me and his hope that it was reciprocated. Instead, I made my comments within the terms of the talking-as-dreaming that I sensed was occurring. I said, "See if this way of putting it squares with what you have in mind. For me, the sound of Cage's voice as he tells his dream at the end is different from the way his voice has sounded at any point earlier in the film. He's not faking a change in himself in order to get Holly Hunter to stay with him. There's a genuine change in who he is. You can hear it in his voice." It was only in the act of saying these words that I recognized that not only was I addressing the imagery of the patient's talking-as-dreaming, but also I was implicitly saying that I could hear and did appreciate the difference in the patient's voice and my own voice, as well as in Cage's voice.

Mr B, with relief in his voice, said, "That's it."

While at that moment in the analysis neither Mr B nor I was inclined to talk more directly about what was happening in the analytic relationship, it was clear to both of us that something new and significant was taking place between us. Some weeks later, Mr B spoke about his experience of that session in which we had talked about *Raising Arizona*. He compared his experience during that session with his experience of reading as a child: "The way I spoke about *Raising Arizona* couldn't have been more different from the way I read as a kid. In reading I became a part of another person's imaginary world. In talking about that film in the way we did, I found that I was not losing myself, I was becoming more myself. I wasn't just talking about what Nicolas Cage and the Coen brothers had done, I was talking about myself and what I thought of those films."

Still later in the analysis, Mr B spoke about that session: "I think that it doesn't matter what we talk about – movies or books or cars or baseball. I used to think that there were things that we should be talking about like sex and dreams and my childhood. But it now seems to me that the important thing is *the way* we talk, not *what* we talk about."

It may be that the film, *Raising Arizona*, caught the patient's imagination because it is a story of two people who, unable to create (dream) a life of their own, attempt in vain to steal a part of someone else's life. But I believe that the emotional significance of the session did not lie primarily in the symbolic meaning of the film; rather, what was most important to the patient and me was our experience of talking/dreaming together. It was an experience in which Mr B was "dreaming himself up" in the sense that he was creating a voice that felt like his own. I think that he was right when, on looking back on the session, he said that it did not matter what we talked about. What was significant was the experience of his coming into being in the very act of dreaming and talking in a voice that felt like his own.

In reading my version of the dialogue that occurred in the session, I am struck by how difficult it is to capture in words the analytic experience of talking-as-dreaming. The dialogue here and throughout this chapter too often manages only to "play the notes" while failing to "make the music" of the intimate, multi-layered exchange that constitutes talking-as-dreaming. That "music" lies in tone of voice, rhythm of speech, "oversounds" (Frost, 1942, p. 308) of words and phrases, and so on. The nature of the music of talking-as-dreaming differs widely from patient to patient and from transference experience to transference experience. In one session, the music of talking-as-dreaming may be the music of an adolescent girl talking to her father at the dinner table after the rest of the family has left. The sound is the sound that the father hears in the voice of his daughter (who is beautiful in his eyes) as she speaks her thoughts on anything in the world she cares to talk about. In another transference-countertransference experience, the sound of talking-as-dreaming is the sound of a three-year-old boy babbling as his mother does the dishes. He speaks in a sing-song way – almost a lullaby – in semi-coherent sentences about the fact that his brother is a jerk and that he loves it when Deputy Dawg flies and that he hopes they will be having corn on the cob again tomorrow, and on and on. And in still another experience in the transference-countertransference, talking-as-dreaming has the heart-wrenching sound of a 12-year-old girl, who after having awoken in tears in the middle of the night, is telling her mother how ugly and stupid she feels and that no boy will ever like her and that she will never get married. It is these sorts of sounds that are so difficult to capture in writing.

## Concluding comments

I will conclude with three observations about talking-as-dreaming. First, in the experience of talking-as-dreaming, even when the analyst is participating in the patient's dreaming, the dream is, in the end, the patient's dream. Unless this fundamental principle is borne in mind, the analysis may become a process in which the analyst "dreams up the patient," instead of the patient dreaming himself up.

Second, when I engage in talking-as-dreaming, it always feels to me as if more, not less, attention to the analytic frame is required. It seems to me that a good deal of analytic experience is required before an analyst can responsibly engage in talking with patients in the ways I have described. In participating in talking-as-dreaming, it is essential that the difference between the roles of analyst and patient remain a solidly felt presence throughout. Otherwise, the patient is deprived of an analyst and of the analytic relationship that he needs.

Finally, in introducing the idea of talking-as-dreaming, I am not making a case for "breaking the rules" of psychoanalysis or for making new rules. Rather, I think of the clinical work that I have described as improvisations which took form in the context of my analytic work with particular patients under particular circumstances. In saying this, I find myself returning to what I believe to be so fundamental to the practice of psychoanalysis: our efforts as analysts to invent psychoanalysis freshly with each of our patients.

# 3

# On psychoanalytic supervision

Psychoanalysis has generated two forms of human relatedness that had not previously existed: the analytic relationship and the analytic supervisory relationship. While Freud discussed the analytic relationship in elaborate detail, curiously, so far as I have been able to determine, he made not a single reference in his *Complete Psychological Works* to supervision or to the supervisory relationship (with the exception of his work with Little Hans's father [1909]). Nonetheless, the supervisory relationship is an outcome of Freud's "discovery" of psychoanalysis and has become integral to the process of becoming a psychoanalyst (both during formal analytic training and in the course of the graduate analyst's ongoing efforts to become a psychoanalyst). The psychoanalytic supervisory relationship is, consequently, an indispensable medium through which psychoanalytic knowledge is passed from one generation of psychoanalysts to the next.

## A theoretical context

I view both the analytic relationship and the supervisory relationship as forms of "guided dream[ing]" (Borges, 1970a, p. 13). In this chapter, I will explore some of the forms such dreaming takes in the supervisory setting. I will make no effort to address the multiplicity of emotional forces at work in the supervisory relationship or to be prescriptive regarding how supervision ought to be conducted. Rather, I will describe several analytic supervisory experiences (one of which is my own experience in supervision with Harold Searles) that are illustrative of different facets of the way in which I think and work as an analytic supervisor. Before presenting four supervisory experiences,

I will briefly discuss a number of ideas that constitute essential aspects of the theoretical framework for my work as an analytic supervisor.

### *Dreaming the analytic experience*

In the tradition of Bion (1962a, 1970), I conceive of dreaming as the unconscious psychological work that the individual does – both while asleep and in waking life – with his lived emotional experience (see Chapter 1 for further discussion of my conception of dreaming). From this perspective, the supervisory experience is an experience in which the supervisor attempts to help the supervisee dream the elements of his experience with the patient that the analyst has previously been only partially able to dream (his "interrupted dreams" [Ogden, 2004a]) or has been almost entirely unable to dream (his "undreamt dreams" [Ogden, 2004a]).

When I speak of "interrupted dreams," I am referring to states of mind in which unconscious thoughts become so disturbing as to interrupt the individual's capacity for thinking and dreaming. For example, nightmares are dreams in which the dream-thoughts are so frightening as to disrupt the dreamer's capacity for dreaming, and consequently the individual awakens in a state of fear. Similarly, play disruptions occur when the thoughts and feelings being experienced in play overwhelm the child's capacity for playing. Neurotic symptoms (e.g. obsessional rumination, phobias, diffuse anxiety states, and so on) also represent types of interrupted dreaming. The patient manifesting this type of symptomatology is able to dream (to do unconscious psychological work) with his lived experience only up to a point. The neurotic symptom marks the point at which the individual ceases to be able to do unconscious psychological work, and in the place of such work a static psychological construction/symptom is generated.

In contrast to interrupted dreams, "undreamt dreams" reflect a virtually complete inability to dream one's lived experience. What cannot be dreamt is foreclosed from unconscious psychological work. Psychically foreclosed (undreamable) experience may manifest itself in a variety of forms, including psychosomatic disorders and severe perversions (de M'Uzan, 2003), night terrors (Ogden, 2004a), split-off pockets of psychosis, dis-affected states (McDougall, 1984), and schizophrenic states of non-experience (Ogden, 1980).

A supervisee's ability to dream his emotional experience with his patient up to a point and no further reflects the fact that the supervisee has been doing some genuine unconscious psychological work with the emotional experience occurring in the analysis, but his capacity to do that work has been disrupted by the disturbing nature of the thoughts and feelings being generated in the analysis. Disruptions of this sort are manifested in large part as a limitation of the supervisee's ability to generate and sustain a receptive reverie state and make analytic use of his reverie experience. He may find, for example, that he is no longer having utilizable associations to the patient's dreams and that he is experiencing a dulling of his associational linkages to what is taking place in the analytic relationship. These psychic states (sometimes associated with actings-in, such as mistakenly ending a session early) usually do not constitute major breaches of ethical conduct or professional responsibility. The analyst, with the supervisor's help, is usually able to take notice of, think about, and make analytic use of what is contributing to the disruption of his waking dreaming. (The first clinical vignette that I will present involves supervisory work in which the supervisee experienced this form of disruption of his capacity to dream his experience with the analysand.)

A supervisee's almost complete inability to dream his experience with the patient is a far more serious matter than his being only partially able to dream what is occurring in the analysis. The supervisee who is unable to dream his experience is often unaware that there is a problem in the analysis and finds it difficult to make use of supervision. The symptomatic manifestations of an inability to dream are usually more treatment-destructive than those associated with interrupted dreaming. An inability to dream the experience being generated in the analysis may take the form of the analyst's decision to declare the analysis a success and then to unilaterally set a termination date (in an unconscious effort to evade facing an analytic impasse). In other instances, the analyst may develop a psychosomatic disorder or a countertransference psychosis. In still other cases, the analyst may commit boundary violations such as engaging in a sexual relationship or a business relationship with the patient or soliciting the patient's active support in realizing the analyst's political ambitions. (In the last of the four clinical vignettes that I will present, I discuss a supervision in which the supervisee's inability to dream the analytic experience was manifested in the form of developing a psychosomatic disorder and a psychotic countertransference experience.)

## *Dreaming up the analysand in the supervisory setting*

A second element of the theoretical context for my work as an analytic supervisor involves re-framing the question, "Who is the patient whose analysis is the subject of the supervision?" The analyst does not bring the analysand to the supervisory session; rather (with the help of the supervisor), the analyst "dreams up" the patient in the supervisory setting. In other words, the patient who is brought to life in the supervision is not the living, breathing person who talks with the analyst in the analyst's consulting room. Rather, the patient who is presented in the supervisory session is a fiction created in the medium of words, voice, physical movements (e.g. the supervisee's hand gestures), irony, wit, unconscious communications such as projective identifications, and so on.

All of the ways that the analyst consciously and unconsciously brings his experience with the analysand to the supervision do not add up to the actual presence of the patient – rather, they issue in the creation of a fiction. By the term "fiction," I am not referring to a lie. Quite the opposite. In the act of presenting a case in supervision, the supervisee "turns facts into fictions. It is only when facts become fictions [that] . . . they become real" (Weinstein, 1998). In this sense, creating the patient as a fiction – "dreaming up the patient" – in the supervisory setting represents the combined effort of the analyst and supervisor to bring to life in the supervision what is true to the analyst's experience of what is occurring at a conscious, preconscious, and unconscious level in the analytic relationship (Ogden, 2003b, 2005b).

## *The interplay of the analytic experience and the supervisory experience*

A third element of the theoretical context for my work as an analytic supervisor involves an awareness of the unconscious interplay of the supervisory relationship and the analytic relationship. Searles (1955) was the first to write about this aspect of the supervisory relationship in "The Informational Value of the Supervisor's Emotional Experiences." In this groundbreaking paper, Searles states:

> The emotions experienced by a supervisor – including even his private, "subjective" fantasy experiences and his personal feelings about the supervisee – often provide valuable clarification of [unconscious interpersonal] processes currently characterizing the relationship between the supervisee and the patient. In addition, these processes are often the very ones which have been causing difficulty in the therapeutic relationship . . . The [conscious and unconscious] processes at work currently in the *relationship between* patient and therapist are often reflected in the [conscious and unconscious] *relationship between* therapist and supervisor (p. 157). . . . I shall refer to this phenomenon as the *reflection process*.[1]
>
> (1955, p. 159, italics in original)

Thus, the unconscious level of the therapeutic relationship is not simply brought to the supervisory relationship in the form of the supervisee's spoken account of his work with the analysand; rather, it is brought to life in the unconscious and preconscious dimensions of the supervisory relationship itself. An essential part of the task of the supervisor and supervisee is to dream (to do conscious and unconscious psychological work with) the interplay of the supervisory and the analytic relationships. Some aspects of this psychological work are put into words by the supervisor and the analyst, while other aspects of this work are left unspoken, or perhaps discussed in a displacement (for example, in the supervisor's speaking of an analogous experience that he has had in his own experience as a supervisee or as an analyst). Each supervisory pair handles the discussion of the relationship between the supervisory relationship and the analytic relationship in their own unique way.[2]

1 The phenomenon referred to by Searles as "the reflection process" has subsequently been termed "parallel process." I find the latter term to be a misnomer in that the relationship between the analytic process and the supervisory process is anything but parallel: the two processes live in muscular tension with one another and are all the time re-contextualizing and altering one another. The analytic relationship and the supervisory relationship constitute two facets of a single set of conscious and unconscious internal and external object relationships involving supervisor, supervisee, and patient.

2 It is beyond the scope of this chapter to review the literature on the interplay of the supervisory relationship and the analytic relationship. Berman's (2000) paper provides both an overview of the subject and insightful observations on the "matrix of [conscious and unconscious] object relations" (p. 276) constituting the analytic supervisory relationship. Other important contributions to this topic include: Anderson and McLaughlin

### *The supervisory frame*

The final element of the theoretical context underlying the clinical discussions that follow involves the "frame" of the supervisory relationship. Analytic supervision requires the same freedoms and protections as the analytic relationship (see Gabbard and Lester, 1995, on boundaries and boundary violations of the supervisory frame). The supervisor is responsible for creating a frame that ensures the supervisee's freedom to think and dream and be alive to what is occurring both in the analytic process and in the supervisory process. The supervisory frame is a felt presence that affords the supervisee a sense of security that his efforts at being honest in the presence of the supervisor will be treated humanely, respectfully, and confidentially.[3] The supervisee entrusts to the supervisor something highly personal – his conscious, preconscious, and unconscious experience of the intimacy and the loneliness, the sexual aliveness and the deadness, the tenderness and the fearfulness of the analytic relationship. In return, the supervisor shows the supervisee what it is for him to be (and to continue to become) an analyst through the way he thinks and dreams, the way he formulates and expresses his ideas and feelings, the way he responds to the supervisee's conscious and unconscious communications, the way he recognizes the supervisee as a unique individual for whom the supervisory relationship is being freshly invented.

## Four clinical illustrations

### *1. Dreaming a patient into existence*

In the first hour of consultation in which Dr M discussed his work with his patient, Ms A, he told me that he had been worried for some

(1963); Baudry (1993); Doehrman (1976); Epstein (1986); Gediman and Wolkenfeld (1980); Langs (1979); Lesser (1984); McKinney (2000); Slavin (1998); Springmann (1986); Stimmel (1995); Wolkenfeld (1990); and Yerushalmi (1992).

3 I find that the supervisory process is severely compromised when it takes place under the aegis of a training program that requires the supervisor to evaluate and report to the training program his impressions of the work of the supervisee. None of the four supervisory experiences that I describe in this chapter took place in the context of a training program.

time about what was happening in the analysis. Ms A had begun analysis because she was chronically depressed and experienced a terrible fear of dying. She had developed a number of somatic symptoms that included rather severe dermatitis.

Dr M told me that the patient said she felt disconnected from her husband and children and worried that while she had managed to "fake it" at work for a long time, she was about to be found out. In describing her childhood, Ms A portrayed her father – who was a teacher and a lay minister – as a man of great intelligence and depth, a person whom she and "everyone who knew him greatly admired." He could also be very harsh, moralistic, and demeaning, and regularly referred to the patient as "dumb as dirt." The patient's mother – a quiet and withdrawn woman – seemed "not to notice much of life outside of her head." (When I quote the patient's words, I am, of course, not quoting the patient, but quoting Dr M's "fiction" derived from his conscious and unconscious experience with the patient. Dr M did not take notes during the sessions with his patient.) Ms A said that throughout every session she felt at a loss to understand why Dr M would continue working with her, given the fact that she was an intolerably boring patient.

Dr M said that, in the course of the first year of this five-session-per-week analysis, he had talked with the patient about his sense that she felt torn apart by, on the one hand, her wish to demonstrate to her father (and now to Dr M) that she is not "dumb as dirt" and, on the other, her wish to be loyal to her father (and to their toxic bond) by proving him right with regard to his judgment that she is a worthless failure who will do nothing with her life. Despite this interpretive work, the patient remained depressed and extremely frightened that she was dying.

About halfway into Dr M's initial consultation session with me, he said, "I'm not sure why – maybe because it feels so primitive – but I'm embarrassed to say that I smell an acrid odor when Ms A is in my office, and it lingers after she leaves. I've made excuses for her in my own mind: maybe she has been to the gym earlier in the day and has not had time to shower." I said to Dr M that I could not recall whether he had told me the patient's age. I was not aware at the time how this question followed from what Dr M had just been talking about. He told me that he was not sure how old she was and had never asked her directly. The longer the analysis went on, the more difficult it felt to him to ask her. He said, "Very often, when I meet Ms A in the waiting room and as she leaves at the end of the session, I find myself staring into her face trying to get a sense of how old she is. Only now as we're talking about it, I think that what I'm doing in looking at her in that way is trying to see in her face what she looked like as a child, and as an adolescent, and as a young woman. At times I see in her face a very pretty, inquisitive, and intelligent young girl or college student."

I asked Dr M what the patient, when she was young, had dreamt of becoming. He told me that she had had considerable talent as a dancer and had been a member of a ballet company for several years after college. She gave up dance when she developed stage fright that she could not overcome. Ms A decided to go to law school "as a default position." Though she had achieved some success in corporate law, the work held no interest for her.

I commented to Dr M that it seemed to me that the patient had not been able to dream herself into being; I thought that her fear of dying (given concrete form in her physical symptomatology) may be a manifestation of her sense that she has never been born in any real emotional sense and fears that she will die before she is born. I added, "This may be a stretch, but I think that the odor that you smell may be the patient's way of bringing to the sessions the smell of her own decaying. What little she feels there is of her is dying right there in your office."

In the initial consultation session being discussed, Dr M had managed to create in the medium of words a "fiction" that brought to life what was true to his emotional experience of Ms A, a patient who could not dream and, instead, somatized her undreamt experience. Dr M had been able to dream some of the dreams that the analysand was unable to dream – for example, his dreaming Ms A as a girl and young woman who was in the process of being and becoming a person in her own right. His dreaming her in the consultation session had been facilitated by my dreaming her in the form of my "out of the blue" question about her age. My dream/question and Dr M's dream of Ms A in her youth stand in marked contrast to her father's "dreaming" her. Her father's "dreams" were not dreams, but virulent projective identifications in which the patient served as a place or a thing into which his disowned, denigrated, "dirty" self was housed (while he held as his own the morally pure aspect of his split sense of self). He needed her to serve this function, and she was frightened of losing her value to him by refusing to play that role. At least she was "some thing" to her father; she felt she was nothing at all to her mother.

In the course of the succeeding months of analysis, the patient told Dr M a dream: "Big chunks of my skin and muscle came off in my hands. When I tried to put the clumps of tissue back on my body, even more came off. It was horrible. It was as if my dermatitis had gone crazy." Dr M said to the patient that he thought that, as odd as it might sound, Ms A had been working in analysis to get her dermatitis to "go crazy" in the sense of changing it from a bodily event into a psychological event, a *feeling* of going crazy, of coming apart that she could think about and talk about with him.

Dr M never brought up with the patient the odor that he had smelled. He told me, "It simply disappeared." Perhaps it disappeared when he and Ms A became able to dream her previously undreamable experience of herself as a decaying corpse (that was in the process of becoming dirt).

## 2. *On the importance of having time to waste*

On my return from a holiday break, Dr W, an analyst who had been consulting with me for many years, began a supervisory session by enquiring about how my time away had been. Not taking this as a pro forma question that invited a mechanical response, I said that one of the best parts of the vacation had been having time to read Don DeLillo's (1997) novel, *Underworld*. It happened that Dr W had also recently read the book. We talked about the way in which the novel had immediately won us over by making metaphorical use of an actual 1951 baseball game between the Giants and the Dodgers. The game was decided by Bobby Thompson's bottom-of-the-ninth home run – which the tabloids called "the shot heard round the world." Though legendary to those who follow baseball, that game was a meaningless event, not only from the perspective of the history of mid-twentieth-century America, but also in relation to other events that occurred the same day. That day, the Russians detonated their second atomic bomb, which was truly a "shot heard around the world." Every character, every event in DeLillo's sprawling 800-page epic, is connected in one way or another (often extremely indirectly) to Bobby Thompson's home-run ball.

Dr W and I talked about how the all-important, and at the same time insignificant, events of our lives – beginning with the accident of our birth – together constitute the infinitely complex, ever-expanding web that we come to experience as who we are. Each of us creates a sense of what is true that is in large part determined by the "lineage" of a feeling – the fluid history of our storied being over time. We spoke also of the structure of the book as a whole, a book that seems to be bursting at the seams as it strains to contain not only an extraordinary assemblage of characters and ideas, but a seemingly endless series of shifts in tone and voice. A sentence from the book came to mind in this regard that I could only paraphrase. Later that day, I found that sentence in the book in which DeLillo describes the crowd emptying from the stadium after the game: "Shouts, bat-cracks, full bladders and stray yawns, the sand-grain manyness of things that can't be counted" (DeLillo, 1997, p. 60).

Dr W and I each had our favorite sentences from the book in which the speaker/narrator offers a knowing phrase concerning why he or another character acted as he or she did, and then punctures the illusion that we can know with any certainty why we feel and behave as we do. Dr W recalled a sentence that read something like, "She slavishly took care of her husband out of a profound sense of guilt – at least that's what she told herself." The narrator seems dogged by the need to be as honest as language allows him to be: he seems to try not to allow exaggeration, nostalgia, euphemism, or any other form of watering down the truth to slip by unnoticed. Of course, he fails, and knows it.

We talked about how the writing captures in an extraordinarily accurate, and yet unselfconscious, way the experience of silently talking to ourselves, sometimes in words, sometimes in shifts in perspective or feeling tone. These are our own doomed efforts at being fully honest with ourselves. Dr W and I spoke about our experiences as analysands in which each of us, in quite different but overlapping ways, had very frequently felt that at least two conversations were going on at the same time: the spoken one with the analyst and the unspoken ones with ourselves. Both Dr W and I became aware, in a way that felt new to each of us, that as analysands she and I had been engaged in multiple layers of conversation, each somehow a commentary on the others, each with its own unique sort of truth and its own brand of self-deception.

Dr W said, "When I spoke to my analyst, there were almost always unspoken counter-thoughts and counter-feelings: 'Do I really believe that?' Or 'I sound like a whiny adolescent.' Or 'His silence has suddenly turned icy. He does that when he's angry . . . or scared.' " She explained that she did not mean that the spoken conversation was a lie or a cover-up, but that when the spoken conversation was given undue authority in relation to the unspoken ones, she had a sense that she had distracted herself and her analyst from the effort to hold the full complexity of what was occurring. In Dr W's analysis, and in my own, the unspoken conversations were not often talked about. Perhaps it was for the best that the unspoken "counter-thoughts" be allowed their underworld life, their dream-life. To attempt to give voice to them all would probably generate an obsessional paralysis of thinking. And yet, it had been unsettling for me when I had felt that my analyst had lost touch with the cacophony of my underworld conversations. In this part of the conversation with Dr W, I was becoming more fully aware of the way in which my underworld – my barely audible dream-life – is a constant presence that gives texture to everything I think and feel. I came to experience my analyst's not drawing attention to my underworld as a form of acceptance of it rather than as an obliviousness to it.

I did not feel that this supervisory session had been "wasted" in talking about a novel. Somehow the pleasure that Dr W and I found in reading the book led to a discussion of our own analytic underworlds. It was only because we were in a frame of mind akin to the analyst's state of reverie (Ogden, 1997a, b) that we could use the supervisory hour in the utterly unexpected way that we did. This sense of having all the time in the world, of having time to waste, to my mind, is a necessary element of the emotional background for an important kind of associative thinking in the analytic supervisory setting. Of course, matters of clinical urgency always take precedence in supervision, but it has been my experience that an analyst's dutiful presentation of clinical material may serve as a defense against a more freely associative form of thinking, a form of thinking and imagining that enhances the range and depth of what can be learned in the supervisory setting.

In writing about the importance of having time to waste in the supervisory setting, I am reminded of an experience that occurred some forty years ago. It was an experience that made a deep impression on me at the time and has influenced the way I view both analysis and analytic supervision. In the fall of my freshman year of college, an English professor speaking to a group of parents was asked by one of the fathers what his job consisted of. The professor said he taught two classes that met for an hour and a half twice a week. The father asked what else he did, to which the professor replied, "Nothing. You see that's what I'm paid to do – nothing. Only if I have nothing to do, do I have the freedom to go to a bookstore and ignore 'the great books' – the works of Shakespeare, Cervantes, Dante, Goethe, Proust, Joyce, Yeats, and Eliot. They and a great many other novelists, playwrights and poets are writers I would read and re-read if I felt I had only a limited amount of time to spend. But because I have time to waste, I am able to buy a book just because I like its title or am intrigued by its opening sentence or by a paragraph a hundred and fifty pages into it. Or I can read the 'lesser' works of Hardy or Conrad or Updike – books that very few people consider to be worth their time. I have time to read anything I like. How else could I happen upon good writers whom I've never heard of, who have never won a prize – even in high school – who don't have a single famous friend to write an ecstatic blurb for the book jacket?"

For me, it is a shame when a supervisor and supervisee never find that they have time to "waste." An important mode of thinking and feeling and learning is lost.

## *3. Dr Searles*

A little more than twenty-five years ago, I wrote to Harold Searles, asking to meet with him while I was in Washington, D.C. He left a message on my answering machine in which he offered a two-hour block of time for our meeting and suggested that I read a paper that he had published in which he discussed his work with a schizophrenic patient whom he refers to in his writings as "Mrs Douglas."

When I arrived at Dr Searles's office, the door to his consulting room was open and he motioned me to come in. He said, "You must be Dr Ogden," and indicated where I should sit. On the table between us was a tape recorder on which a large reel of tape was in place. It was already clear that there would be no words of welcome, no polite enquiries into what I was doing in Washington, no small talk at all. He told me in a matter of fact way that he had been taping every session of the five-session-per-week analysis with Mrs Douglas for more than 20 years.

We listened together for about five minutes (which felt like a very long time). Dr Searles told me that he had grown to love Mrs Douglas despite her best efforts to infuriate him. He said, by way of example of her keenly perceptive ways of provoking him, that she had recently decided not to go on a day-long outing organized by Chestnut Lodge where she was an inpatient. He believed that she had somehow sensed that he was desperate to use the 50 minutes of the session she would have missed to work on a paper that he was close to completing. He pressed the button to start the tape again and eased back in his chair to listen. About 10 minutes into the recorded session, Dr Searles (in the session with Mrs Douglas) said to the tape recorder (as if it were a third person in the room along with him and Mrs Douglas), "The first Dr Searles has just left the room and a second Dr Searles has entered." In speaking these words to the tape recorder, his voice had the sound of a theatrical aside spoken by an actor to the audience in the middle of a conversation with another character in the play. But it did not seem to me that his comment was meant to be humorous. He seemed to have a need to talk to someone, anyone, even an imaginary third person. There was an oversound of sadness and resignation in his voice in response to being seen not as a whole person, but as a parade of parts of people who were constituted more by means of the patient's projections than by her perceptions of who he was and how he felt about her.

Some time later (time had become analytic time as opposed to clock time), I noticed tears rolling down Dr Searles's face. I did not feel surprised by this, given how rapidly and thoroughly social artifice had been dispensed with. I remained silent and felt no need to say or do anything in response. We continued to listen for a while longer. Dr Searles then said that no doubt I had seen him weeping. He told me that the time spent with me had reminded him of the recent death of Ping-Nie Pao, an analyst at Chestnut Lodge who had been a close friend of his for many years. He said that there were very few people left in his life – and he suspected very few left in the world – who would want to spend time listening to a tape recording of a session from the twenty-first year of an analysis of a schizophrenic patient. Dr Searles's comment, like almost everything else that he said and did during the time we spent together, had a quality of unguarded intimacy. There was something both freeing and frightening about what was occurring. I was being wordlessly invited to experience and speak from an unconscious level and to enter into, and simultaneously observe, a dreamscape without knowing where the dreaming was heading – we never do know where a dream is going.

I told Dr Searles that listening with him to the session had led me to feel an odd combination of feelings that I only now recognized as a feeling that I often experienced in my work with a blind schizophrenic man. I explained that I was at the time a full-time therapist on the staff of a long-term analytically oriented inpatient ward. I said that in my work with the blind patient, I had a sense that there was nothing to be afraid of because everything horrific that could happen had already happened. It was as if the world had already been destroyed and had no future and so it did not even occur to either of us to hide from one another. There was nothing courageous about feeling that way – it did not arise out of a feeling of having conquered fear, but from a sense of utter defeat. Dr Searles said he lived with that feeling most of the time, and added, "People sometimes mistake it for arrogance, but it's not – it's the opposite of arrogance."

We listened some more as one Dr Searles after another arrived and left the room in the recorded session. I told Dr Searles that the patient I had mentioned often ended his sentences with the "reassuring" words, "Nothing personal." Searles laughed deeply – the kind of laugh that is a release of an entire lifetime of feeling that includes a sense of welcome connection with another person (with me, for the moment, and with Ping-Nie Pao, and I don't know who else) and also of unspeakable disconsolate recognition of the impossibility of making a reliable connection with Mrs Douglas and with his own schizophrenic mother (whom he had mentioned several times in the course of our meeting). In the course of the consultation, we moved fluidly between discussing my analytic work with two schizophrenic patients and Dr Searles's analysis of Mrs Douglas. I felt dazed when I left Dr Searles's office. I have not until now written down my recollections and impressions of that meeting.

What this supervision with Dr Searles represents for me, now as I look back on it, is a form of bringing the entirety of oneself, the full depth and breadth of one's emotional responsiveness, to bear not only on an analytic relationship but also on an interaction between supervisor and supervisee. In the experience with Dr Searles, it did not seem to matter whether it was his or my own conscious, preconscious, and unconscious responsiveness that took the lead at any given moment as we talked about our analytic work and what was happening between us. Claims of "ownership" or credit due for originality or insightfulness held no purchase. All that seemed to matter was making a human connection and gaining a sense of what was true to the present moment, both of the analytic work and of the supervisory work. As I mentioned earlier, there was a dream-like quality to the consultation. In part, this was because primary process linkages were honored. But as important was the fact that the effort to be honest with ourselves was at every moment shaping the experience. That experience of guided dreaming with Searles reflected the way in which dreams cannot lie – they may disguise, but they are incapable of being dishonest.

### *4. A nightmare from which the analyst could not wake up*

Dr L, an analyst who had been in weekly supervision with me for about three years, told me that her analytic work with a pediatrics nurse was so disturbing that she did not think that she could continue working with the patient. This state of mind was highly unusual for Dr L, whose work had been consistently thoughtful and steady, even while in the grip of intense transference-countertransference dilemmas. The patient, Ms B, had consulted Dr L because she felt continually "on the edge of going crazy." Despite the fact that she was morbidly obese (she weighed more than 400 pounds at the beginning of the analysis), she insisted that her "freedom to eat" not be interfered with.

Ms B had told Dr L that over a span of years in childhood her parents had frequently given her enemas. She initially described the enemas as extremely frightening, but in the course of the analysis, admitted to herself and to Dr L that the enemas also became a source of sexual excitement. Anal masturbation, which had begun during the period of the enemas, continued to the present as the patient's exclusive form of sexual activity. During both the enemas and the anal masturbation, the patient felt as if she were "dissolving."

Toward the end of the second year of the analysis, Ms B spontaneously began a diet that resulted in a 240-pound weight loss over a period of fourteen months. When, according to the diet regimen she was following, the patient reached her normal weight, she began to experience anxiety of an intensity that she had never previously felt. The patient's already very limited capacity for self-reflective thought and her ability to remember her dreams all but disappeared. Ms B filled the sessions with detailed accounts of her work as a nurse. She described in a tone of voice saturated with thinly disguised pleasure the details of catheterizing the bladders of small children. She described the procedures as "unfortunate necessities." Some months later, after being transferred to a pediatrics neonatal unit, Ms B one day spoke of the "beauty" that she had seen in a mother's holding in the palms of her hands her tiny, deformed premature infant. Dr L found Ms B's description of this mother and infant particularly upsetting. It felt to Dr L that the patient was taking perverse delight in the terrible pain that this mother was feeling.

Dr L, in the course of the years that we had worked together, had told me that she had completed a pediatrics residency before becoming a psychiatrist and then a psychoanalyst. She had also told me that her oldest child had died of a lymphoma when he was ten years old after lengthy treatment with chemotherapy. Dr L was of course aware that her feelings associated with her son's illness and death were a source of anger, sadness, and revulsion in response to Ms B's accounts of her experiences as a nurse. Despite this self-awareness, Dr L found that the effect on her of what Ms B was doing in the analysis rendered her unable to think.

As Dr L was describing her recent experiences with her patient, my mind wandered to a supervision during my first year of psychiatric residency. I was presenting a patient who had come to the clinic because of terrible headaches. Over the course of a few sessions, it turned out that the patient's wife had ordered him out of their bedroom. My patient slept in the bed of his eight-year-old son, while the son slept in the patient's bed with the patient's wife. I told the supervisor that family therapy was impossible because the patient's wife was agoraphobic and could not leave their house. The crusty supervisor asked me what I would do if I were walking down the street and saw a house on fire. I said that I probably would call the fire department. He said, "No, you'd go in to see if you could help anyone get out." He told me to arrange to meet with the patient and his wife and child at their house. I worked with them each week at their house for more than a year. After only two sessions, the son returned to his own bedroom and the patient to his. Much more gradually, the wife's agoraphobia diminished in intensity, and the son made friends for the first time in his life.

Refocusing on the conversation with Dr L, I said that it seemed that the patient's self-hatred embodied in her obesity (making herself grotesque while slowly killing herself) and her insistence on maintaining her "freedom to eat" had served to give the patient a feeling of some degree of control over her savage, primitive hatred of her mother. Moreover, I felt that the patient was unconsciously fused with ("dissolved in") her mother. A psychotic transference had developed in which Dr L had become, in the patient's mind, the undifferentiated conglomerate of herself and her mother. I told Dr L that I thought that she was experiencing a countertransference psychosis in the form of feeling inhabited and taken over from the inside by the patient. Dr L said that this formulation made sense to her. But in the succeeding weeks, she continued to find it almost unbearable to be in the same room with Ms B.

I began to suspect – in part as a consequence of the reverie involving my own experience in supervision – that I was afraid of getting fully involved with what was happening in the supervision and in the analysis of Ms B. I had been busy calling the fire department instead of going into the burning house. I could then see that both the supervisory situation and the analytic situation required decisive interventions. I told Dr L, "I think that unconsciously, and perhaps consciously, Ms B knows or, more accurately, in a primitive way smells the fact that you have cared for a dying child of your own. The patient feels that she is in a position to get inside of you and torture you in the most brutal way possible, just as she had felt that her parents had gotten inside of her and malignantly took her over." I went on to say that Ms B's savage assaults were highly destructive to herself, to Dr L, and to the analysis, and that they had to be put to an end. Dr L then told me that she had for some time felt that the effect of the patient on her was so destructive that it would literally kill her. She said that she could feel her blood pressure rise to levels that felt dangerously high during the sessions and had on several occasions taken extra medication for her hypertension prior to her meetings with Ms B. (Dr L had found that her blood pressure was in fact significantly elevated above her regular baseline following her sessions with Ms B.)

Speaking more freely now, Dr L said that she felt utterly helpless with the patient because she could not tell Ms B not to talk about her work (which constituted practically the entirety of the patient's life). I said to Dr L that that was exactly what she had to do: to tell the patient that her accounts of her work with sick children and their parents were serving not as communications about distressing aspects of the patient's life, but as attacks on Dr L (which replicated the attacks Ms B had experienced as a child). I added that I felt that it was essential that Dr L say to the patient in her own words that from here on she will be asking the patient not to continue to give descriptions of her duties and interactions at work and, instead, to describe the feelings that her life experiences evoke in her. I said that I expected that Ms B would act as if she had no idea what Dr L was talking about when Dr L spoke of the patient's "attacks" on her and that Ms B would argue that it is impossible to talk about her feelings without talking about the events that elicited them. I suggested that a possible way of responding to such retorts would be to say, "All you can do is do your best, and I will let you know when you cross the line."

In disbelief, Dr L said, "You mean I can tell her not to talk about her work – about what she does to those children and her perverse distortions of what the parents of the children are feeling? For weeks now I've been having dreams in which I'm in my office with Ms B and am yelling at her, 'Get out, get out!' My husband has had to wake me up from these nightmares. He's told me that I have been thrashing around yelling, 'Get out, get out.'"

I said to Dr L, "You feel trapped in a never-ending nightmare with the patient: there is no escape, just endless fear and pain. Nightmares ordinarily wake us up and, in so doing, release us from experiencing dream-thoughts that are too painful to bear and too painful to work with unconsciously." Dr L, both in her sessions with Ms B and in her sleep at night, had become more a figure in a dream than the dreamer of the dream (a dreamer of the analytic relationship). She understood that in her work with Ms B she would have to be the one to wake herself up and wake up her patient from the endless nightmare being played out in the sessions.

The analysis changed markedly after Dr L put a stop to the patient's disguised sadistic attacks on her. Dr L began to interpret the psychotic transference in which the patient and her mother were merged and projected into Dr L where the fused mother-patient was tortured. Also, after the attacks were put to an end, Dr L told me that she no longer experienced elevation of her blood pressure during or after her sessions with Ms B. In this period of supervision, there was a complex interplay of the unconscious levels of the supervisory relationship, the analytic relationship, my own reverie experience, and the supervisee's external and internal worlds. Dr L had needed help from me to awaken herself from the unending nightmare that she was living with Ms B. Only then could she begin genuinely to dream her experience in the analytic relationship.

Several months later, Dr L told me that Ms B was neither attempting to torment her nor being passively compliant; rather, for the first time in this ten-year analysis, Ms B was showing interest in her inner life, including the reasons why she had for so long been torturing Dr L.

## Concluding remarks

In sum, the role of the psychoanalytic supervisor is to facilitate the supervisee's work of dreaming aspects of the analytic relationship that the supervisee has previously been unable to dream. Since the original analytic situation cannot be brought to the supervision, the work of the supervisory pair involves "dreaming up" the patient, creating a "fiction" that is true to the analyst's emotional experience with the analysand. Such dreaming takes place within the context of a supervisory frame that safeguards the analyst's freedom to think about and be alive to all that is happening in the analytic and supervisory relationships, as well as in the dynamic interplay between the two. It is important that at least occasionally the supervisor and supervisee feel that they have "time to waste." Such a state of mind allows for a less structured, more freely associative type of thinking that is akin to the analytic state of reverie. Thinking of this sort often generates fresh perspectives on what the supervisor and analyst felt they "already knew."

# 4

# On teaching psychoanalysis

Psychoanalytic teaching at its best opens a space for thinking and dreaming in situations in which the (understandable) impulse is to close that space. To fill that space as a teacher is to preach, to proselytize, to perpetuate dogma; not to fill it is to create conditions in which one may become open to previously inconceivable possibilities. With regard to teaching clinical psychoanalysis, a central goal of analytic teaching is the enhancement of the analyst's capacity to dream those aspects of his experience in the clinical situation that he has not previously been able to dream.

The observations concerning analytic teaching that I offer in this chapter are drawn primarily from my experiences in teaching two weekly seminars, each currently in its twenty-seventh year. I will begin by describing the setting in which I have taught and then will discuss the following four aspects of analytic teaching that I have found to be of particular importance in conveying what I view as essential qualities of psychoanalysis: (1) a way of reading analytic writing; (2) clinical teaching as a form of collective dreaming; (3) reading poetry and fiction as experiences in "ear training"; and (4) the art of learning to forget what one has learned.

## The setting

In 1982, I began to teach two weekly hour-and-a-half seminars at my home. I co-led one of these with my colleague and friend, Bryce Boyer, until his death in 2001. Both seminars are open-ended and continue year-round. The format of the seminars has changed minimally over the decades. Three or four consecutive seminar meetings in which a paper is discussed alternate with three or four meetings in which a seminar member presents current analytic work with one of his or her patients. During the clinical meetings, the presenter reads process notes from the most recent session or two, and includes as much reverie and other countertransference experience as he or she is comfortable in providing.

The membership of the seminars has become quite stable. The tenure of the ten to twelve members of each seminar is, on average, longer than five years. The open-ended nature of the seminars, in combination with the lengthy tenure of the participants, confers a quality of timelessness to the seminars. There is a sense of having all the time in the world to follow a case or read a paper or follow a tangent (as long as it remains interesting and productive). What we do not get to one week, we will get to the next, or perhaps the week after that.

Everything about the seminars is voluntary. The groups are not associated with any training program; no certificate of participation is awarded; no one is required to present a case or even to enter into the discussions. The seminar members are free to leave the seminar at any time without explanation and, as far as I have been able to determine, without being viewed as disloyal to the group or as a failure. A number of people have left the seminar after several years of participation and have returned a decade or so later. Others have attended the seminars for only a few sessions or a few months before deciding that the level of discussion, the group process, or some other quality of the seminar did not suit them.

The make-up of the seminars has varied over time, but there is always a wide range of levels of clinical experience and mastery of psychoanalytic theory among the members. While the large majority of seminar members have been in clinical practice for at least fifteen years, there are always some participants who are quite new to the field. Of late, almost all of the members of one of the seminars have completed formal analytic training, while few of the members of the other seminar have done so. Despite this difference, I find that both the liveliness and the level of sophistication of the discussions that take place in the two groups are comparable.

## A way of reading analytic writing

In the course of the decades of reading analytic texts in the seminars, I have become increasingly aware of the inseparability of an author's ideas and the way he or she uses language to present those ideas. Having thoughts is quite a different phenomenon from speaking one's ideas, and speaking one's ideas is quite different from presenting those ideas in writing. An analytic paper must not only include original thinking, it must "work" as a piece of writing and as an experience in reading. To simply discuss a paraphrased version of some of the ideas developed in an analytic paper is to lose touch with the fact that the paper is a piece of writing. The words, syntax, voice, sentence and paragraph structure, and so on, together contribute to the effects created and the ideas conveyed in the medium of language. Consequently, for the past nine or ten years, it has seemed to me that when studying an analytic paper or book, it is not only preferable, but essential, to read the paper aloud in the seminar, sentence by sentence, paragraph by paragraph. To do otherwise feels to me equivalent to studying a short story exclusively by means of recounting the plot.

Reading texts such as Freud's (1917) "Mourning and Melancholia," Winnicott's (1945) "Primitive Emotional Development" or Berger and Mohr's (1967) *A Fortunate Man* has required two or three months of weekly seminars for each; reading Bion's (1962a) *Learning from Experience* took most of a year. It quickly became apparent in reading papers and books in this way that good writing can stand the test of being read aloud; mediocre writing cannot.

My experience in leading the seminars in close reading of texts is reflected in a series of papers that I have written over the course of the past decade (Ogden, 1997c,d, 1998, 1999, 2000, 2001a,b, 2002, 2003a, 2004b; see also Chapters 7 and 8). These papers have shaped and have been shaped by the close readings that we have done in the seminars. (For me, teaching and writing are inseparable: I write what I teach and teach what I write.)

I have consistently found that reading a text aloud, sentence by sentence, has profoundly altered the nature and quality of the discussions that take place in the seminars. It feels to me that we are not simply discussing an author's ideas, but immersing ourselves intellectually and emotionally in the way the author thinks/writes, how he talks, what he values, who he is, who he is becoming, and, perhaps most important, who we are becoming as a consequence of the experience of reading the work together.

When the writing is good, the author creates in the experience of reading something like the phenomenon that he is discussing. Here, and in subsequent sections of this chapter, I will attempt not simply *to tell* the reader about how I go about teaching psychoanalysis, but *to show* the reader something of how I teach. For example, in reading aloud Loewald's (1979) "The Waning of the Oedipus Complex," one can hear the tension between Loewald, the earnest classical Freudian, and Loewald, the revolutionary. Loewald does not see the Oedipus complex as a process of internalizing parental prohibitions in the face of the threat of castration; rather, he sees the Oedipus complex as the fantasied and, as I will discuss, actual murder of the oedipal parents carried out in the process of the child's emancipating himself from parental authority.

For Loewald, revolting against and appropriating the authority of the parents underlie the child's establishment of a sense of self that is responsible for himself and to himself. Oedipal parricide is followed, in health, by atonement for the murder and the restitution to the parents of their (now transformed) authority as parents of a child who is increasingly autonomous. Thus the Oedipus complex, for Loewald, is most fundamentally a battle between parents and children that mediates the succession of generations (see Chapter 7 for a close reading of Loewald's 1979 paper).

One can hear in the sound of Loewald's words and sentences his own "urge for emancipation" (p. 389) from the conventional psychoanalytic wisdom of his time:

> If we do not shrink from blunt language, in our role as children of our parents, by genuine emancipation we do kill something vital in them – not all in one blow and not in all respects, but contributing to their dying. As parents of our children we undergo the same fate, unless we diminish them.
>
> (Loewald, 1979, p. 395)

In this passage, there is an assemblage of powerful monosyllabic words (which is unusual for Loewald): shrink, blunt, role, kill, fate. We can hear and feel in these words – earthy, Anglo-Saxon words – the ongoingness of the body's pulse, the matter-of-factness of one event following the next in the living of everyday life. The experience that is created in the language captures something of the at once ordinary and extraordinary process of the succession of generations, of the movement of life and responsibility from one generation to the next. That movement of responsibility is taking place in the very experience of reading in the form of the passage of ideas from one generation of analysts to the next, from Freud to Loewald, from Loewald to the reader.

In reading aloud in the seminars the last section of Loewald's "The Waning of the Oedipus Complex," it was clear that Loewald's sentences had become confusing, not because the ideas being presented were of greater complexity, but because the language being used was less lucid. For example, in discussing analytic work with borderline patients, Loewald states, "It is as though, in comparison, the neurotic conflicts commonly encountered are, as viewed from this uncommon ground, blurred reflections, garbled echoes of a basic quest those patients desperately pursue in pure culture" (pp. 399–400). The sentence structure here is painfully contorted. It took me many readings to begin to glean a sense of what Loewald is saying, and even then it seemed that many of the words are poorly chosen. For example, is "uncommon ground" ground not held in common by neurotic patients and borderline patients? And why does Loewald use the phrase "garbled echoes," a phrase that suggests that the conflict experienced by the borderline patient echoes (derives from) neurotic conflict? What is the logic of a developmental sequence that seems to place the origins of neurotic conflict prior to that of borderline psychopathology? (It is clear from the context that Loewald does not subscribe to such an idea.)

I think that the breakdown of language in this portion of Loewald's paper reflects a breakdown in his thinking. Writing, after all, is a form of thinking. Loewald, up to this point in the paper, is daring in his willingness to deviate from both classical Freudian thinking and American ego psychology. Earlier in his article, Loewald proposed that a healthy (universal) "psychotic core" (p. 400) of the individual is "an active constituent of normal psychic life" (p. 403). This conception of the importance of the archaic, undifferentiated dimension of the Oedipus complex constitutes a radical break from the widely held notion that the Oedipus complex and its "heir," the superego, are definitive of neurotic and healthy (well-differentiated) psychic structure.

Despite the earlier clarity of his thinking in this regard, Loewald, beginning in the murky sentence under discussion, retreats from his unconventional, original thinking and embraces the mainstream thinking of his time: "in the classical neuroses it [the psychotic core] may not need specific analytic work" (p. 400). This contradicts his previously stated notion that the psychotic core is an inherent part of the Oedipus complex and, it would seem, is always a part of a thorough analysis of the Oedipus complex. Could Loewald really believe that patients suffering from "classical neuroses" may be, to all intents and purposes, unencumbered by psychopathology manifesting itself in forms such as "problems of primal transference in analysis, complexities of transference-countertransference phenomena, and of direct communication between the unconscious of different persons" (p. 399)? The response of one of the seminars to Loewald's "retreat" was an audible groan: it felt to the group that Loewald had undermined his own original and creative thinking which had breathed new life into the Oedipus complex. It was as if Loewald had broken his word to the reader – a promise to say what he believes to be true despite internal and external pressures to do otherwise. I believe that this strong emotional response from the seminar members derived at least in part from the way in which reading a paper aloud in a group setting creates quite an immediate sense of personal connection between the group and the writer.

Another example of the seminar's intense response to the language of the papers being read aloud occurred in a discussion that took as its starting point Loewald's (1979) idea that in emancipating ourselves from our parents, "we do kill something vital in them – not all in one blow and not in all respects, but contributing to their dying. As parents of our children we undergo the same fate, unless we diminish them" (p. 395). In the course of discussing this portion of the paper, a seminar member spoke of the extremely painful and immediate fear of death that she felt during the years after she outlived the age at which her mother died. She went on to describe the way in which the experience of having grandchildren had not eradicated the feeling, but had transformed it. She now felt that her life is not only an experience of making something but, as importantly, an experience of making room for someone and something else. "My aging and the process of my dying now seem to have a purpose, a use – which makes dying less frightening to me. If I had read Loewald's paper ten years ago . . . What I was about to say isn't true. I have read this paper many times over the past fifteen to twenty years, but it hasn't touched me in the way it has this time – reading and listening to it and talking about it here. I have been able to hear in Loewald's writing the voice of a parent teaching me how to be a parent in my current stage of life."

Another seminar member then commented, "I think the word *contributing* in that sentence refers to more than our children playing a role in pushing us along – pushing us off the edge of a cliff to our deaths – as they seize authority from us. The word *contributing* suggests to me that our children *give* us something of value in the sense of helping us to learn how to grow old and die, how to be alive to ourselves in the process of aging and dying."

A third member of the seminar remarked that the transfer of authority to the next generation is not simply a loss. She described the sense of freedom she experienced in no longer being responsible in the same way for the lives of her children. "It is as if a debt has been paid. Growing old isn't only a matter of parents making room for children to become responsible adults, it is also a matter of children, in taking responsibility for themselves, making room for their parents to be alive and free in a new way."

Several others in the seminar who had young children spoke of dreading the time when their children would be leaving home. They feared that after their children left home, they, as parents to their children, would not have a "real" life with their children, but only the remnants of one; this would leave them feeling terribly empty. An older member of the group said that these fears, unfortunately, were well founded: he had found that while there is greater freedom for parents when children leave home, in his experience, that freedom did not begin to compensate for the loss of vitality and joy that he experienced in life: "There is nothing, for me, remotely like being transported into the world that we enter when we see things through the eyes and ears and words and voice of a child." In response, I quipped, "God, in his infinite wisdom, created adolescence. No one can bear the thought of parting from the dear souls that our children are when they're 6 years old (particularly as we watch them sleep). But, fortunately, they become lunatics at 12 or 13, and by the time they're 16 we begin to count the days until they vacate the premises. If it weren't for adolescence, we'd never let them go. In this sense, we kill our adolescent children, we contribute to ending their lives *as children*, and in so doing, help them grow up."

Such responses to Loewald's paper, one might argue, are not necessarily the product of reading his work aloud and discussing it line by line. That argument, in the abstract, is irrefutable. But, for me, the fact remains that my experience in teaching Loewald's 1979 paper without reading it aloud had generated discussions that were far less emotionally intense and intellectually rich than the experience I have just described.

## Clinical teaching as collective dreaming

I view psychoanalytic clinical teaching as a form of collective dreaming that occurs when a seminar group is "a going concern" (Winnicott, 1964, p. 27). The members of the seminar, individually and collectively, enter into a form of waking dreaming in which the group helps the presenter to dream aspects of his clinical experience that he has been unable to dream on his own. A group unconscious is constructed (a form of "the analytic third" [Ogden, 1994]), that is larger than the sum of the unconscious minds of each participant, while, at the same time, each participant retains his own separate subjectivity and his own personal unconscious life. In what follows, I describe a psychoanalytic seminar group engaged in the process of learning and teaching by means of collective dreaming.

Dr R began her clinical presentation of an analysis that was in its third year by saying that she found the analysand, Ms D, "fascinating," "intriguing," and "a clinical challenge." The patient had been in analysis for most of her adult life and said that she had found each of the analyses to be "helpful." (The words in quotation marks are Dr R's rendering of her own and the patient's words.)

The patient grew up in an upper-middle-class family that appeared to the outside world to be "perfect," while in fact both of her parents were "closet alcoholics." They would get drunk every evening and then would viciously attack one another verbally, with particular emphasis placed on the other's sexual inadequacy. Often, they would, unexpectedly and for no apparent reason, turn their venom on the patient. By the time the patient was five or six years old, she had learned to retreat to her room where she would turn the television up to maximum volume or put on earphones and "blast loud music into her head."

As I listened to the opening few minutes of Dr R's presentation, I had a disturbing feeling – primarily in the form of a knot in my stomach. As I thought about it, I became increasingly unsettled by Dr R's use of the words "fascinating," "intriguing," and "clinical challenge." It seemed to me that there was a disjuncture between these rather clichéd words and what she was describing. The patient's use of the word "helpful" to describe her previous analyses was so insipid as to feel to me like a mockery of her analyses, past and present. These empty words being used by Dr R and the patient felt so unexpressive and evasive as to be maddening. I experienced a fleeting thought/

image of being a helpless, passive member of an audience watching something barbaric performed on stage.

I told Dr R that I had an uneasy feeling about the analytic scene that she was describing. I said that even though she found the patient "fascinating," there seemed to me to be an undercurrent of something else that felt like the other side, the dark side, of the "helpfulness" of all of the previous analyses. A seminar member said that she, too, had had the feeling that "something else" was happening. She said that Dr R's voice sounded different as she presented this case. "I can't describe the difference, maybe I'm just imagining it. I don't know. But you don't sound like yourself." There followed a silence in the seminar that lasted almost a minute (which is very unusual).

Dr R, seemingly ignoring what had just been said, commented: "The patient is a very bright, extremely well-read woman who can talk with great insightfulness about novels, poetry, film, art exhibits, and so on. Her dreams, too, are elegant and seem to convey highly nuanced states of mind. So, in a way, everything is going well. But she does such a good job of it that I find that I have nothing to add. During sessions with her, several times I have found running through my mind a comment made by an analyst during my residency as he was presenting an analytic case of his own. His patient seemed to be conducting the analysis by herself. One of the residents asked how the analyst felt about that. The analyst said, 'It's fine with me, so long as she does a good job of it.' I was bothered by the glib quality of his answer. He didn't seem to want to think about what it meant that he was being so thoroughly excluded from the analysis. A year or so later, I heard that the patient had committed suicide."

Dr R then, in a somewhat mechanical way, presented more "background material," including an account of the patient's many physical illnesses. Ms D had had kidney stones once or twice a year for a decade, in part because of chronic heartburn for which she took antacid tablets "like a chain smoker." The patient said that her doctor felt that surgery would probably be necessary to remove a large stone from her right kidney which intermittently blocked the flow of urine from that kidney. Dr R interrupted herself and said that she had become increasingly anxious, almost panicky, as she was presenting this part of the patient's history. She said that it was as if her mind had stopped working. "I can't tell what's real about the patient. It seems possible that all of what I've just said about her may be a series of stories that she's invented. I feel as if I don't know what's real about her and the analysis and what's not." A wave of anxiety and concern swept over the group in response to Dr R's distress.

A member of the seminar said to Dr R that he had felt increasingly anxious as she was speaking of the patient's physical illnesses. He said that he had been reminded of the film, *The Invasion of the Body Snatchers*. He felt as if Dr R's words were not communications of feelings and ideas, but were like spores that were infecting him and would grow in him like the patient's kidney stones, but with a diabolical quality as if they had a life of their own. He said he felt trapped in the room as he listened to her and had to stifle the impulse to leave.

I said to Dr R that I thought that what she was feeling was related to the reverie that she had described in which the analyst had been unable to recognize the way in which he was being obliterated by the patient. That analysis seemed to represent for Dr R the catastrophic outcome of an analyst's inability to hear what a patient is trying to say without words.

Dr R said that she worried a great deal about the work with Ms D. She had not been able to sleep deeply for the past several months and had lain awake ruminating about what she had said and what she should have said to Ms D in that day's session.

I told Dr R that I imagined that when she had been told that she did not sound like herself, she had felt alarmed. "The idea of not being yourself (not speaking with your own voice) is, I think, a very disturbing one to entertain. It is a state that feels like being taken over by someone else. I suspect that the terror of being taken over is a feeling that Ms D felt as her drunken parents lacerated each other and then her. The patient, as a child, had done everything she could to disconnect herself not only from her parents, but also from herself and her feelings (for example, by blasting deafening music into her ears)." Dr R responded by saying that she could feel her anxiety draining away as she listened to what I was saying.

At the beginning of the next seminar meeting, Dr R said that she had had a dream the previous night. "In the dream, I was in a crowded place. I don't know where it was. I was holding my daughter's hand. She was about three in the dream. All of a sudden I realized that she was gone. I hadn't been aware of letting go of her hand, but she wasn't there. I was terrified and called out her name as loudly as I could. At some point, a couple brought her back. I knew that they had taken good care of her, but she looked very frightened. I hugged her and hugged her, but we both could not stop trembling." Dr R said that she had not realized how frightened she had been for some time that she was losing her mind and her self in the work with Ms D. It seemed to her that the couple in the dream was the seminar group. She added that even though there was great relief in feeling that she had retrieved herself (with the help of the group in the previous seminar meeting), the whole experience had left her feeling very shaky.

The psychological movement in the first of the meetings I have described occurred in the space of about an hour of "clock time," but timelessly in "dream time." The members of the group, individually and collectively, participated (consciously and unconsciously) in helping Dr R dream the experience that was being generated in the analysis of Ms D. My comments to Dr R, in response to her experience of not being able to think or to know what is real, drew heavily on the seminar's collective waking dreaming. These "dreams" included my own momentary waking dream of helplessly and passively watching something barbaric unfold; a seminar member's experience of Dr R's voice as not that of Dr R; and the reverie involving the body snatchers substituting something inhuman for what had been human.

The collective dreaming that took place in the seminar (which I organized and tried to put into words) was of help to Dr R in dreaming on her own an aspect of her analytic work that she had previously been unable to dream. A part, but only a part, of that dreaming process took the form of Dr R's dream in which she lost herself and was helped by a couple to reconstitute herself. The dream did not entail a manic flight from either the patient's or the analyst's lived experience. The dream encompassed the full complexity of the emotional situation, including the fact that the horror of having lost oneself can never be eradicated; rather, that horror lives on as a part of who one is (as represented by the trembling that continued after Dr R was reunited with her daughter).

The process that I have described is one in which a group participated in dreaming an aspect of a clinical experience that an analytic colleague had not been able to dream on her own. To my mind, this process lies at the core of psychoanalytic clinical teaching.

## Reading poetry and fiction as a form of "ear training"

For many years, poetry and other forms of imaginative writing have been essential to the dream-life of the analytic seminars that I have conducted. Devoting seminar meetings to reading and discussing a poem or a work of fiction has served multiple purposes. The pleasure to be had in reading good writing and discussing how the piece works as writing is an end in itself. At the same time, reading poetry and fiction in an analytic seminar is an experience in "ear training" (Pritchard, 1994) – that is, the refinement of one's capacity to be aware of and alive to the effects created by the way language is being used. This may take the form of developing one's ear for the subliminal expressiveness of the sounds and "oversounds" (Frost, 1942, p. 308) of words; for the compacting of disparate meanings in ambiguity and metaphor; and for "the feats of association" (Frost, quoted by Pritchard, 1994, p. 9) achieved in the medium of rhythm, assonance, consonance, alliteration, and so on.

These ways in which language works also constitute a principal medium in which patient and analyst communicate their thoughts and feelings to one another. For example, in a previous contribution (Ogden, 2003b), I discussed a patient who, prior to our first session, paced for several minutes in the passageway leading to the door to my waiting room. Despite my having given him specific directions, he could not decide which of the two doors was the waiting-room door. Most of the initial meeting was spent talking about this experience. Toward the end of the session, the patient said, "Out there, I felt so lost" (p. 604). How different the effect created by the patient's statement would have been had he said, "I felt very lost out there." The patient's way of stating his experience had the effect of isolating the "Out there" aspect of himself (and that part of the sentence) from the rest of the sentence; then the words "I felt so lost" brought those feelings – the experience of being lost – into the room with me, into the analysis. I do not believe that the patient intentionally constructed the sentence in this way in order to create the effects it achieved; rather, I believe that the structure and movement of his conscious and unconscious emotional experience shaped the way he unselfconsciously structured the sentence.

Of the many experiences of ear training that have occurred in the course of reading poetry and fiction in the seminars, the reading of two short stories collected in William Carlos Williams's (1984a) *The Doctor Stories* stands out in my mind. Williams was not only one of the major American poets of the twentieth century, he was also a full-time doctor who practiced in a poor, rural area of New Jersey in the 1920s, 30s, and 40s. (All of *The Doctor Stories* are fictional but clearly draw on Williams's experience as a doctor.) One of my favorites of these short stories, "The Girl with a Pimply Face," begins:

> One of the local druggists sent in the call: 50 Summer St., second floor, the door to the left. It's a baby they've just brought from the hospital. Pretty bad condition I should imagine . . . Going up I found no bell so I rapped vigorously on the wavy-glass door-panel to the left . . .
>
> Come in, said a loud childish voice.
>
> I opened the door and saw a lank haired girl of about fifteen standing chewing gum and eyeing me curiously from beside the kitchen table. The hair was coal black and one of her eyelids drooped a little as she spoke. Well, what do you want? She said. Boy, she was tough and no kidding but I fell for her immediately. There was that hard, straight thing about her that in itself gives an impression of excellence.
>
> I'm the doctor, I said.
>
> Oh, you're the doctor. The baby's inside. She looked at me. Want to see her?
>
> Sure, that's what I came for.
>
> (Williams, 1984b, pp. 42–43)[1]

As I read this passage aloud in the seminar, several members of the seminar smiled, one roared with laughter. Each word of these sentences is as hard-edged and, at the same time, as winning as the doctor and the girl in the story. (The voice of the narrator *is* the story – nothing the least bit interesting is happening at the level of plot in these sentences.)

Williams, in the opening lines of his "case presentation," sets a standard for us as analytic writers and as presenters of analytic cases. The members of the seminar listened, keenly aware of the skill, experience, and labor entailed in using language to convey so precisely who the patient is and who the doctor is at each moment in this encounter. Williams's patient is "a lank haired girl of about fifteen standing chewing gum." The sound of the words *lank haired* conveys all the sense of adolescent slouch – a studied droop that speaks volumes

[1] By William Carlos Williams, from *The Collected Stories of William Carlos Williams*, copyright © 1938 by William Carlos Williams. Reprinted by permission of New Directions Publishing Corp.

of disdain without saying a word or moving a muscle (except for the methodical chewing of gum and the droop of an eyelid). At the same time, the girl, despite herself, is curious about the doctor, a curiosity hidden in her demand that he justify his taking up room in her life: "Well, what do you want? She said." (Williams does not use quotation marks, which has the effect of blurring the distinction between the spoken and the merely thought, and the distinction between himself and the girl in whom he clearly sees himself. He is instantly attracted to her and she to him: "Boy, she was tough and no kidding but I fell for her immediately." We, as readers, fall for both of them immediately.

Not only are characters being dreamt up by Williams in the writing, and by the reader in the experience of reading, the world the girl inhabits is also being brought to life. That world is a world of emotional poverty and isolation – the girl, not an adult, meets the doctor who has come to attend to a very sick, perhaps dying, infant. And yet, there are sparks flying between this pair. The lank haired girl and the doctor show not the slightest inclination to allow the poverty and isolation of her world to deaden them. All of this is contained in a few tightly coiled words and sentences.

Words in this story, as in analytic writing, are not ornaments, nor are they packages in which information is transported from writer to reader. Words in a story – whether it be a work of fiction or an analytic narrative (which, as discussed in Chapter 3, is also necessarily a fiction) – *create* experiences to be lived by the reader (see also Ogden, 2005b). The writing does not re-present what happened; it creates something that happens for the first time in the experience of writing and reading. Few writers are better able than Williams to teach us something about how this is done, if we, as analytic writers and case presenters, are willing to allow him to teach us by attending closely (listening keenly) to what he is doing and how he is doing it.

Another of *The Doctor Stories*, "The Use of Force" (Williams, 1984c), creates in the writing the emotional complexity involved in the forceful interventions doctors (and analysts) make in the course of their clinical work. Again, the power of this story lies in the voice of the doctor/narrator, and it is in that aspect of the writing that the opportunity for ear training is most rich. *The Doctor Stories*, as a whole, and this story, in particular, seem to be a form that Williams has invented in an effort to talk to himself about disturbing aspects of his life as a doctor. The narrator's voice in this story is that of a doctor being torn apart emotionally as he attempts to get a throat culture from a frightened girl who may have diphtheria:

> . . . I said, come on, Mathilda, open your mouth and let's take a look at your throat.
>
> Nothing doing . . .
>
> I had to smile to myself. After all, I had already fallen in love with the savage brat; the parents were contemptible to me. In the ensuing struggle they grew more and more abject, crushed, exhausted while she surely rose to magnificent heights of insane fury of effort bred of her terror of me.
>
> (Williams, 1984c, pp. 57–58)[2]

What kind of doctor talks like this? What is happening in the voice of the narrator? Is this a doctor who hides from himself by using Philip Marlowe-style narration of his life? If not, in what ways is the voice more complex, more interesting, more engaging, more tortured than that of Marlowe?

In this passage, the reader, too, is being asked to look at his own savagery which he recognizes in himself in his role as parent, spouse, friend, analyst, and so on. It is a savagery that feels inescapable if one is to carry out one's responsibility as a doctor, and yet, a source of horror, shame, and remorse. If I am honest with myself, it is a savagery that I have acted out with every one of my long-term patients – for example, by too often being a little late in beginning the sessions in the analysis of a patient who had suffered extraordinary neglect as a child.

The voice of the narrator is not a preaching voice, nor is it a confessional one. It is the voice of a man intent on being honest with himself. The narrator's honesty is itself savage: "She fought, with clenched teeth, desperately! But now I also had grown furious – at a child. I tried to hold myself down but I couldn't" (Williams, 1984c, p. 59). The narrator's recognition of the full force of his fury is followed by a change in his voice: "I know how to expose a throat for inspection" (p. 59). There is a self-justifying tone here, almost pleading for respite from his emotional attacks on himself. But the unspoken

[2] By William Carlos Williams, from *The Collected Stories of William Carlos Williams*, copyright © 1938 by William Carlos Williams. Reprinted by permission of New Directions Publishing Corp.

plea in his voice is not compelling. It is a "doctorly" voice that has removed itself from the emotional situation: "I know how to expose a throat for inspection. And I did my best" (p. 59). The "savage brat" has become "a throat."

The reader/listener can hear in the voice of the doctor a need (which by now has taken on a life of its own) to defeat the child (no longer the illness) at any cost: "We're going through with this" (p. 59). There is far more of the truth of what is happening in the sound of this voice than in the doctorly rationalization that preceded: "I did my best."

But a subliminal shift in the savage voice of the doctor is taking place, a shift that renews our interest in arriving at a fuller response to the question, "What kind of doctor talks like this?" Williams continues: "The child's mouth was already bleeding. Her tongue was cut as she was screaming in wild hysterical shrieks" (p. 59). It is no longer "the tongue" that is bleeding, but "her tongue." "Perhaps I should have desisted and come back in an hour or more" (p. 59), and then, dispensing with the evasive word *perhaps*, he goes on: "No doubt it would have been better" (p. 59). The voice speaking this last sentence has been changed by the experience of talking to himself in the process of writing the story. The sentence is not one of raw self-condemnation. The rhythm of the words slows here, as if the speaker has stopped to take a breath: "No doubt it would have been better." The words are simple (all but one are monosyllabic) and the sounds of the words are soft, devoid of hard consonants.

But this is not the end of the internal struggle – life is never so simple: "But I have seen at least two children lying dead in bed of neglect in such cases, and feeling I must get a diagnosis now or never I went at it again" (p. 59). The self-justifying invocation of children "dead of neglect" rings a bit hollow to the reader and to the narrator/doctor: "But the worst of it was that I too had got beyond reason. I could have torn the child apart in my own fury and enjoyed it. It was a pleasure to attack her. My face is burning in it" (p. 59).

Now he has said it all – and it had to be said in its entirety. The pleasure was already so patently, disturbingly present in the language that if it were not said plainly, straightforwardly, there could be no genuine resolution (even if the "resolution" can only be a "momentary stay" [Frost, 1939, p. 777]). The "success" involved in the doctor's finally prying open the girl's jaws, seeing the diphtheria membrane on her tonsils, and getting a throat culture is not only life-saving in intention, it is also born of frenzied, murderous fury. The story closes: "Now truly she *was* furious. She had been on the defensive before but now she attacked. Tried to get off her father's lap and fly at me while tears of defeat blinded her eyes" (p. 60). The question, "What kind of doctor speaks this way?" has become all the more richly layered and complex. No wonder analytic patients fly at us after we have prematurely put into words something that for most of their lives has been unconscious. What has been unconscious has been so for good reason. Literal or metaphorical "tears of defeat" well up in the analysand's eyes when we know too much too soon and cannot keep it to ourselves (Winnicott, 1968).

Bion (1962a) observed that the analyst must listen to himself listening. I would add that the analyst must also listen to himself speaking and, in so doing, be continually asking himself, "What kind of doctor talks like this?" "Who am I when I speak to this patient in this way?"

Listening well to oneself requires not simply a thorough analysis and ongoing scrutiny of the countertransference, it requires "ear training." It is for this reason that I view reading poetry and fiction in an analytic seminar not as a dalliance or as a break from "real" analytic reading, but as an indispensable part of teaching psychoanalysis.

## The art of learning to forget what one has learned

Teaching psychoanalysis is no less an art than is the practice of psychoanalysis. We learn the art of psychoanalytic teaching to a very large degree from those who have been our teachers. An experience with one of my own psychoanalytic teachers that occurred more than thirty years ago remains very much alive in me.

While working at a university hospital in England, I participated in a Balint group for a period of about a year. The group was composed of seven National Health Service general practice physicians (GPs) and a group leader, Dr J, who was a psychoanalyst and consultant psychiatrist in the National Health Service. The group met for two hours weekly and continued for a period of two years. The purpose of the group was to help the doctors become better able to think about the psychological dimensions of their work with their patients. GPs in England at that time saw patients (usually without pre-arranged appointments) in their surgeries in the mornings and went on rounds to the homes of housebound or bedridden patients in the afternoons.

It was recognized that many (perhaps most) patients who consulted their GPs did so not primarily for the purpose of being treated for a physical illness. Without being aware of it, they were going to their doctors in hopes of talking with them about an emotional problem. It was for this reason that the GPs in England who participated in Balint groups felt the need to learn more about how to talk with their patients about psychological difficulties, particularly when the patient was ostensibly consulting them about a physical problem. The seven GPs in the group – five men and two women – were all in their mid-thirties to mid-fifties. My role was that of a "participant observer" who, along with the group leader, commented (in ordinary, non-technical language) on the emotional dimension of the clinical experiences presented by the GPs. I was in my late twenties, only a few months out of psychiatric residency, and clearly the member of the group who had the most to learn about becoming a doctor.

Each week Dr J would begin the meeting by saying, "Who's got a case?" and each week the members of the group would respond with self-conscious silence, all looking at their shoes, trying to avoid eye contact with Dr J. After a minute or so, one of the doctors would describe a recent experience with a patient. In one of these meetings, Dr L, a GP in his early forties, said that a patient of his had left a message saying that her elderly mother (also his patient) had died in her bed. Dr L, an hour or so later, went to "have a look." He briefly examined the elderly woman and confirmed that she was dead. Dr L said that he then called for an ambulance to take the mother to the mortuary. Dr J asked, "Why did you do that?" Dr L, surprised by the question, replied, "Because she was dead." The group, too, was taken aback by Dr J's question. Dr L stared querulously at Dr J for a moment before Dr J asked, "Why not have a cup of tea with the daughter?" Identifying with Dr L, the other GPs and I had thought that common sense would dictate that the doctor, in that situation, would make the necessary arrangements for getting the mother's body to the mortuary. The feeling of being with the daughter in her flat with the mother's body lying in the next room became real for the group in a disturbing way – a corpse is a frightening thing unless one has deadened oneself to the experience. We, as a group, fell silent and simply lived for a period of time with the imagined felt presence of the mother's lifeless body.

Dr L (and the rest of us in identification with him) had shifted into an operational mode in order to get the mother's body out of there as quickly as possible. It had not occurred to any of us to ask ourselves why the daughter was alone with her mother's body when the doctor arrived? Did she have no husband, no children, no family to call? Or had she simply wanted to be alone with her mother for a while? Perhaps she was waiting for the doctor with the hope that he would spend some time with her and her mother's body.

To "have a cup of tea" is to keep possibilities open, to allow to happen whatever will happen. To have a cup of tea is to allow the event to remain timeless for a while and to allow the daughter to dream – to do unconscious psychological work with – the experience (with the help of the doctor). "Why not have a cup of tea with the daughter?" – such an ordinary question, such an act of respectfulness to the daughter, such a simple, human way of being a doctor to this woman and her mother.

The experience in the Balint group that I have just described was one in which Dr L and the other members of the group were learning to forget (more accurately to overcome) what we felt we knew about being a doctor. In this instance, what had to be overcome was the numbing automaticity of the procedures that we have for dealing with "the deceased."

More broadly, this experience has contributed to my viewing analytic learning as biphasic. First, we learn analytic "procedures," for example, how to conceive of, create, and maintain the analytic frame; how to talk with a patient about what we sense to be the leading edge of the patient's anxiety in the transference; how to make analytic use of our reverie experience and other manifestations of the counter-transference. Then, we try to learn how to overcome what we have learned in order to be free to create psychoanalysis anew with each patient. These "phases" are in one sense sequential in that we have to know something before we can forget/overcome it. But, in another sense, particularly after we have completed formal analytic training, we are continually in the process of learning and overcoming what we have learned.

The experience in the Balint group that I have described has stood as a model of analytic teaching for me. The feeling (palpable sensation) that Dr J's question, "Why not have a cup of tea with the daughter?" evoked in me, as I look back on it, was that of a clearance created in which there was time – dream time – in which people may be able to live and dream an experience together. What can happen in that clearance is unique to the situation and to the people living it.

The experience that occurred in the group that day has affected far more than the way I respond to death and grieving. I find that the idea of "Why not?" has become central to the way I think and speak with patients. So often, I find myself asking the patient, "Why not?" "Why not feel frightened or sad or jealous?" "Why not keep to yourself the dream you find so embarrassing?" "Why not leave the session early?" These are not rhetorical questions. "Why not?" is an inquiry into the history of the patient's ways of thinking and feeling which have helped him to stay alive and maintain as much sanity as he could afford under the circumstances.

In sum, teaching psychoanalysis is a paradoxical affair: someone who is supposed to know teaches someone who wants to know what it means not to know.

# 5

# Elements of analytic style: Bion's clinical seminars

For some years now, it has seemed to me that important aspects of my way of practicing psychoanalysis are better described as an analytic style than as an analytic technique. Though style and technique are inseparable, for the purposes of the present discussion, I am using the term *analytic technique* to refer to a way of practicing analysis that has been, to a large extent, developed by a branch or group of branches of one's analytic ancestry, as opposed to being a creation of one's own. By contrast, *analytic style* is not a set of principles of practice, but a living process that has its origins in the personality and experience of the analyst.

The term *analytic style*, as I am using it, puts as much emphasis on the word *analytic* as it does on the word *style*. Not every style that an analyst may adopt is analytic, and not every way of practicing psychoanalysis bears the unique mark (the "style") of the analyst. The idea of analytic style places greater emphasis than does the concept of analytic technique on the role of (1) the analyst's use of, and capacity to speak from, the unique qualities of his personality; (2) the analyst's making use of his own experience as analyst, analysand, parent, child, spouse, teacher, student, friend, and so on; (3) the analyst's ability to think in a way that draws on, but is independent of, the analytic theory and clinical technique of his analyst, supervisors, analytic colleagues, and analytic ancestors; the analyst must learn analytic theory and technique so thoroughly that one day he will be able to forget them; and (4) the responsibility of the analyst to invent psychoanalysis freshly (to rediscover psychoanalysis) with each patient.

The analyst's style is a living, ever-changing way of being with himself and the patient. The entirety of the analyst's style is present in every session with every patient. And yet, particular elements of his style play a greater role than others with any given patient in any given session. Analytic style infuses the specific ways the analyst conducts himself in the analysis. Style shapes and colors method, and method is the medium in which style comes to life.

My thinking about analytic style has been strongly influenced by Bion's work. Of all of Bion's published contributions, the "Clinical Seminars" (1987), for me, provide the richest and most extensive access available to Bion, the clinician. In the present chapter, I will offer close readings of three of the clinical seminars. I will describe what I view as Bion's unique analytic style, and in so doing, illustrate what I mean by the idea of analytic style.

In the decade between the publication of his last major psychoanalytic work, *Attention and Interpretation* (1970), and his death in 1979, Bion conducted two series of clinical seminars: 24 in Brasilia in 1975, and 28 in São Paulo in 1978. In these seminars, in addition to the analyst who presented a case to Bion, there were six or seven other seminar members, as well as a translator. The seminars were tape-recorded, but it was not until 1987 that the collected, transcribed, and edited version was published. I believe that despite the fact that in the seminars Bion is the supervisor and group leader, the "Clinical Seminars" nonetheless afford the reader a rare opportunity to view Bion, the clinician, at work. As will be seen, even though Bion is not the analyst for the presenter's patient, he is the analyst for the patient being "dreamt up" in the clinical seminar. (As discussed in Chapters 3 and 4, I view the patient presented in analytic supervision or in a clinical seminar as a "fiction," an imaginary patient, dreamt up by analyst and supervisor [or presenter and seminar group], as opposed to the actual person with whom the analyst converses in his consulting room.) In addition, in the clinical seminars, Bion does analytic work both with the presenter and with the seminar group.

## Three clinical seminars

### *1. A patient who feared what the analyst might do (Brasilia, 1975, Seminar No. 1)*

The seminar opens with the following exchange:

> Presenter: I would like to discuss a session I had today with a thirty-year-old woman. She came into the consulting room and sat down; she never lies on the couch. She smiled and said, "Today I won't be able to stay sitting here." I asked her what that meant; she said she was very agitated. I asked her what she considered as being very agitated. She smiled and said, "My head is dizzy." She said her thoughts were running away, running over one another. I suggested that when she felt like that she also felt that she was losing control of her body. She smiled and said, "Perhaps; it looks as if that were true." When I continued, suggesting that when her mind was running away like that, her body had to follow her mind's movements, she interrupted me, saying, "Now, don't you try to make me stand still."
>
> Bion: Why should this patient think that the analyst would *do* anything? You cannot stop her coming or send her away; she is a grown woman and presumably therefore free to come and see you if she wants to; if she doesn't want to, she is free to go away. Why does she say that you would try to stop her doing something? I am not really asking for an answer to that question – although I would be very glad to hear any answer that you have – but simply giving an example of what my reaction is to this story.
>
> (pp. 3–4)[1]

Bion inquires, "Why should this patient think that the analyst would *do* anything?" This question to the presenter is, for me, quite startling and more than a bit odd. Of the innumerable aspects of the clinical material presented, why is Bion asking about why the patient would think that the analyst would take action? Only after considerable reflection did it occur to me that Bion is suggesting that the presenter ask himself: "What kind of thinking is the patient engaging in?" "Why is she thinking in this particular way?" Bion is drawing attention to the fact that the patient is engaged in a very limited sort of thinking in which elements of experience that might (under other circumstances) be transformed into thoughts and feelings are, in this instance, being experienced and expressed in the medium of action. The analyst's thoughts are being treated as actions (active forces

[1] Unless otherwise indicated, all page numbers in this chapter refer to "Clinical Seminars" (Bion, 1987).

emanating from the analyst) that hold the power to get the patient to do (not think) something.

So the question, "Why should the patient think that the analyst would *do* anything?" is, at its core, a question concerning the way in which the patient is attempting to handle the emotional problem of the moment and, perhaps, of the entire session: her fear that she is losing her mind.

The patient's evacuation of her unthinkable thought (her fear that she is going mad) has precipitated a rift with external reality in the form of the delusional belief that the analyst is trying to do something to her – that is, "to make me stand still." If the analyst is too frightened to take seriously the patient's statement that she believes in a very concrete way that he is trying to *do* something to her, he will compound the patient's problems by failing to think/dream (to do conscious and unconscious psychological work with) the patient's delusional experience (Bion, 1962a).

Bion, in "simply giving an example of what my reaction is to this story," is giving an unobtrusive interpretation to the presenter. The presenter offered the patient a verbally symbolized thought that he hoped would help her think about her own experience: "I suggested that when she felt like that [i.e. that her thoughts were running over one another] she also felt that she was losing control of her body." The patient responded by smiling and saying, "Perhaps; it looks as if that were true." Her smile (the mention of which has a chilling effect on me) is followed by a statement that seems to offer qualified ("Perhaps") agreement. But the words, "it looks as if that were true," in combination with her smile, seem to me to convey the idea that the analyst sees only what *appears* to be true, and not what is in fact true to what the patient is experiencing.

The analyst ignored the patient's response and repeated his interpretation. The patient interrupted the analyst's repetition of his interpretation by saying, "Now, don't you try to make me stand still." She might as well have said, "Stop doing that to me. Stop trying to make me into you by putting your ideas into my head and in that way controlling my actions (making me stand still). If that happens, I won't be able to move my own mind at all." Bion, in asking why the patient would think that the analyst would *do* anything, is, I believe, trying to help the presenter understand this aspect of the patient's psychotic thinking.

The presenter responds at a superficial level to Bion's question

("Why should the patient think that the analyst would *do* anything?") by saying,

> I was interested to know why she had said "Don't try to keep me still". She said she didn't know the answer to the question, so I suggested that she was preoccupied by my being quiet, still. She said that she did not regard me as being still, but as dominating my movements, my mind controlling my body.
>
> (p. 4)

The presenter's inability to use Bion's question/interpretation reflects, I believe, his fear of recognizing (thinking) the full extent of his patient's psychosis. Because the patient cannot differentiate mind from body (and herself from the analyst), her saying that she experienced his mind as dominating his body was, I believe, equivalent to her saying that she experienced *his* mind as dominating *her* body and mind. In other words, he was relentless in his effort to get into her mind and make her *do* things ("make me stand still" mentally and physically).

Bion tells the seminar:

> I would like to make a guess here as to what I would say to this patient – not in the first session but later on. "We have here these chairs, this couch, because you might want to use any of them; you might want to sit in that chair, or you might want to lie on that couch in case you feel that you couldn't bear sitting there – as you say today. That is why this couch was here when you first came. I wonder what has made you discover this today. Why is it only today you have found that you may not be able to sit in that chair; that you may have to lie down or go away?" All that would be much more appropriate if she had discovered it at the first session. But she was too afraid to discover it.
>
> (pp. 4–5)

This, at first, seems like a very strange thing to say. But I view it as a reflection of Bion's analytic style. Only Bion could have said this. If someone else were to say this, he would be imitating Bion. So what is Bion doing here, or, to put it in different terms, how is Bion being Bion-the-analyst here? He is treating the encounter as if it were the first encounter between him and the patient. He recognizes that the patient is predominantly psychotic and speaks to her from that vantage point (thereby recognizing who she is at that moment). For Bion (1957), the psychotic aspect of the personality is a part of the self that is unable to think, to learn from experience, or do psychological work.

In Bion's imagined conversation with the patient, he speaks to "the non-psychotic part of the patient's personality" (Bion, 1957), the part capable of thinking and doing psychological work. Bion begins by naming in the simplest, most literal terms the objects that are in the consulting room (which are swirling with uncontrolled meaning for the patient because she is frightened and unable to think): "We have here these chairs, this couch, because you might want to use any of them." Bion, in this way, not only tells the patient what the objects are – as external objects – he also tells her implicitly that they are there for her to use as analytic objects, objects that may be used in dreaming up an analysis, if she wishes to try to do so (with his help). He continues: "you might want to sit in that chair, or you might want to lie on that couch in case you feel that you couldn't bear sitting there – as you say today." Here, Bion tells the patient that he thinks that she may be frightened of using the chair today. I believe that Bion is implicitly speculating imaginatively that the chair, for the patient, is a psychological place that once held magical power to protect her against what she fears would happen if she "really" were in analysis. The chair, for some reason, has lost its power today. She might want to use the couch (i.e. she may want to try to become the analytic patient who she had hoped to become when she first came to see the analyst). Bion is not trying to do something to her or to get her to do something – for example, to use the chair or the couch; he is attempting to help her to "dream herself into existence" as an analysand and dream him up as an analyst who may be able to help her to think: "That is why the couch was here when you first came." (See Chapter 1 for a discussion of the idea of dreaming oneself into existence.)

Bion, in a way that is characteristic of him in the "Clinical Seminars," frames his inquiry in the form of the question, "I wonder what has made you discover this today?" That is, "How have you discovered that this is the emotional problem that is most important for you to solve in today's session?" He is implicitly adding that *he* does not have a solution to the problem, but that *she* may, and that he may be able to help her understand something of the problem that is disturbing her, but which she, as yet, is unable to think. Further, what Bion is implicitly saying might be phrased as follows: "In your saying, 'Today I won't be able to stay sitting here,' you are telling me that you are afraid that you can no longer get help here – you fear that you have become so mad ("dizzy") that you have lost hope of being able to become a patient who may be able to make use of me as your analyst."

Bion continues to wonder aloud: "[So] why is it that only today you have found that you may not be able to sit in that chair; that you may have to lie down or go away?" Bion's interpretation (ostensibly to the patient) is perhaps more an interpretation to the presenter: the presenter had not recognized or spoken to the patient about her fear of not being able to be a patient in analysis, a fear she expressed both in her stated inability to use either the chair or the couch and in her statement that the analyst seems to the patient to be able to perceive only what "looks as if . . . [it] were true." It now seems clearer to me why I find the patient's smile so chilling: it bespeaks the enormity of the emotional disconnection that the patient was experiencing between the degree of her emotional distress and her very limited ability to think/dream it, and between herself and the analyst.

Not long after making this interpretation to the "dreamt-up" patient (and also to the presenter), Bion says, "As the analyst, one hopes to go on improving – as well as the patient . . . If I knew all the answers I would have nothing to learn, no chance of learning anything . . . What one wants is to have room to live as a human being who makes mistakes" (p. 6). This, too, is a fundamental element of Bion's style in the "Clinical Seminars." Though, time and again, Bion surprises the presenter and the reader with his uncanny way of sensing the importance of, and making analytic use of, seemingly insignificant elements of what is happening in a session, he no less frequently states, without contrived humility, that an analyst must "have room to live as a human being who makes mistakes." Only in this state of mind is one able to learn from experience: "If you had been practicing analysis as long as I have, you wouldn't bother about an inadequate interpretation – I have never given any other kind. That is real life – not psycho-analytic fiction" (p. 49).

Before turning to the next seminar, let me draw the reader's attention to an implicit element of Bion's clinical approach in this seminar and in a great many others that constitutes an important aspect of Bion's "method." The question that Bion asks the presenting analyst far more often than he asks any other question is: "Why is the patient coming to analysis?" (See, for example, pp. 20, 41, 47, 76, 102, 143,

168, 183, 187, 200, 225, and 234.) It seems to me that in each instance that Bion poses this question, he is implicitly asking the presenter to think of the patient as unconsciously bringing to each session an emotional problem for which the patient has been unable to find a "solution" (p. 100) – that is, a problem with which he has been unable to do psychological work. The patient is unconsciously asking the analyst to help him to think the disturbing thoughts and feelings that he is unable to think and feel on his own. Though Bion, in the seminar just discussed, does not explicitly ask the presenter why the patient is coming to analysis, it seems to me that Bion implicitly raises that question several times. The first instance occurs almost immediately in the seminar when he says, "she is a grown woman and therefore presumably free to come and see you if she wants to; if she doesn't want to, she is free to go away."

### 2. *A doctor who was not himself (Brasilia, 1975, Seminar No. 3)*

This seminar is quite remarkable in the way that it generates a conversation that affords Bion the opportunity not only to put into words, but also to demonstrate so much of his conception of what it means to be an analyst. What is more, Bion does so without using a single technical term. This is consonant with his insistence that we speak to our patients in "words that are as simple and unmistakable as possible" (p. 234), in everyday language, "ordinary articulate speech" (p. 144), and that we, as analysts, talk to one another in the same way.

The analysand being presented is a 24-year-old hospital physician who has been unable to work for four months. He told the analyst, "I came to the consulting room but I stopped. I couldn't stay here. I took the elevator, not feeling well I thought it would be too difficult to come to the session. I thought that if I stayed here I would die" (p. 13). The presenter says that the patient then changed the subject and began to describe his attempt to return to work the previous day despite intense anxiety.

Bion asks, "Was he physically ill?" (p. 13). Once again, Bion's question seems odd, this time because it seems so literal-minded. (There is something surprisingly pragmatic about Bion's way of listening to the presenters' accounts of their work with their patients throughout the "Clinical Seminars.") Perhaps, in asking whether the patient was physically ill, Bion is pointing out that the patient, even though he says that he was afraid that he was dying, has come to see an analyst, not a doctor of internal medicine. It must be that his experience to this point in analysis has led him to feel that the analyst has helped him and that he and the analysis may be of further help to him.

The presenter responds only to the most superficial level of Bion's question by saying, "He thought so [i.e. the patient was consciously aware only of feeling physically ill] but in fact he was suffering an anxiety crisis" (p. 13). Bion is unfazed by the presenter's seemingly not having understood the observation that was implicit in his question. This event, though of no great significance in itself, reflects a critical quality of Bion's style as a supervisor and (I surmise) as an analyst: he "speaks past the presenter." That is, he speaks to that aspect of the presenter that is able to think – the thinking aspect of the personality, which Bion, in his theoretical writings, at times calls "the non-psychotic part of the personality" (Bion, 1957), and, at other times, "the unconscious." It is this aspect of the personality that is capable of making use of lived experience for purposes of psychological work and growth. I use the terms "speaking past the patient," "speaking to the unconscious," and "speaking to the non-psychotic part of the personality" interchangeably in referring to the analyst's act of speaking to the aspect of the patient that is capable of thinking. Since the conscious aspect of the presenter's mind, in the instance being discussed, is not fully able to think, Bion must speak "directly" to the presenter's unconscious or non-psychotic aspect of personality. (See Grotstein, 2007, for a discussion of talking to the patient's unconscious.)

A member of the seminar then asks whether it might "not be interesting to interrupt the patient at this point? I feel there is too much material" (p. 14). Bion responds by saying that he would wait to say something until he had "a clearer idea of what he [the patient] was up to" (p. 14). He adds,

> it's just a suspicion working in my mind – that this patient is one of those people who take up medicine because they are so frightened of some catastrophe or disaster. He can then converse with other doctors and thereby hear about all the diseases there are. Then he won't die, or disasters won't happen, because he is the doctor, not the patient.
>
> (p. 14)

The patient, even though he has qualified as a doctor, is not a doctor because he has no idea about how to genuinely become a doctor – that is, how to develop a sense of coming into being as a person who is able to use his mind to help people (including himself) who are ill.

The same seminar member repeats his question in a slightly different form: "Is this suspicion of yours one of those things the analyst should keep to himself, or could he tell the patient?" (p. 14). Bion makes an interpretation meant for the seminar member, but couched as a statement concerning the patient. He tells the seminar member that people can only do psychological work with a bit of their lived experience and, in particular, analysts early in their career often feel deluged by frightening experiences with their patients:

> A common manifestation of this sort of thing happens when medical students go to the dissecting room to learn anatomy. They break down; they can't go on with it because it causes such an upheaval in their views and attitudes if they dissect the human body.
>
> (p. 14)

Bion, I believe, is saying that he suspects that the seminar member feels compelled to interrupt the flow of thinking (dissecting) in the seminar for fear of breaking down in the analytic "dissecting room" (the clinical seminar). Bion's style of interpretation is highly respectful of the seminar member's defenses as well as his dignity. The thinking that Bion is offering is there to be used if and when the seminar member is ready to make use of it. Without shaming the seminar member, the interpretation seems to have been utilizable by him – his unconscious fear of what he might find out in the seminar was diminished to the point that he was able not to make further interruptions of the analytic work that was occurring in the seminar.

Immediately following Bion's response to the seminar member just described, the presenter says, "I have the feeling that the patient didn't change the subject – he only apparently changed it" (p. 14). Here the presenter is contradicting his own statement made only a few moments earlier. I believe that in the interim he made psychological use of the interpretation that Bion made to the seminar member – that is, that the analyst's anxiety may prevent him from listening to what the patient is unconsciously trying to communicate regarding his fears.

Bion replies to the presenter:

> This feeling of yours is where the interpretation comes from . . . When you begin to feel that all these different free associations are not really different ones, because they have the same pattern, then it becomes important to wait until you know what the pattern is.
>
> (p. 14)

The presenter responds:

> In a seminar with a training analyst, the analyst told me that every good interpretation should contain three elements: a description of the behaviour of the patient; the function of the behaviour; and the theory which is behind the behaviour.
>
> (p. 15)

The reader can almost feel Bion's blood coming to a boil – not in response to the presenter's anxiety, but in response to the arrogance of an analyst who believes that he knows how to do psychoanalysis and believes that, if his supervisees see things as he does, they, too, will know how to do psychoanalysis. Nevertheless, Bion's response is a measured one, but not completely bleached of his feeling that a supervisory style of the sort described is destructive to the supervisee's efforts to become an analyst. At the same time, Bion is fully aware that he is not hearing the ideas of the training analyst (about whom Bion knows nothing), but the ideas and feelings of the presenter who, like his own patient, has momentarily retreated from being a thinking doctor (an analyst) into a passive patient who cannot think for himself.

> Bion: In a sense these theories, such as the one you mention, have a use for the particular person who mentions them. [Bion does not identify that person as the training analyst because he is not addressing that person. He is addressing a split in the presenter's personality in which one aspect of him (who uses analytic theory as a way of not thinking) belittles another aspect of himself (who is trying to become a thinking analyst).] Some of them [analytic theories] will also mean something to you. [The thinking aspect of the presenter may, at times, be able to think about analytic theories and find them useful to him in developing his own ideas.] While you are trying to learn, all these things are very confusing. [Being confused is a state of mind to be experienced as opposed to being evacuated

> and replaced by a feeling that one knows how to do analysis because one has been told how to do so by someone in authority.] This is why I think you can [Bion does not say, "one can"] go on too long with training and seminars. It is only *after* you have qualified [as an analyst] that you have a chance of becoming an analyst. The analyst you become is you and you alone; you have to respect the uniqueness of your own personality – that is what you use, not all these interpretations [these theories that you use to combat the fear that you are not really an analyst and do not know how to become one].
>
> (p. 15)

Bion is demonstrating for the presenter, the seminar members, and the reader what a genuine analytic conversation sounds like. Interpretations do not announce themselves as interpretations. They are a part of "a conversation" (p. 156) in which ideas are stated tactfully, respectfully (often as conjectures), in everyday language. It is becoming clear here that what Bion means by interpretation is not a statement designed to provide verbal symbolization for repressed unconscious conflict in an effort to make the unconscious conscious. Rather, an interpretation is a way of telling the patient a portion of what the analyst is thinking in a form that the patient may be able to use in thinking his own thoughts.

The reader of this seminar can hear with his or her own ears the sound of a person who is able to speak from the uniqueness of his personality and experience. No other analyst sounds remotely like Bion. In a series of papers, I have offered close readings of works by Winnicott, Freud, and Bion (Ogden, 2001a, 2002, 2004b), and will present close readings of papers by Loewald and Searles in Chapters 7 and 8. Each of these analysts speaks/writes/thinks in a way that reflects the uniqueness of his personality. It would be very difficult, even in reading a short passage, not to recognize their distinctive voices.

The analyst's ability to speak with humility from the uniqueness of his personality, from his own "peculiar mentality" (p. 224), lies at the core of what I am calling the analyst's style. It must be apparent by now that style is the opposite of fashion; it is also the opposite of narcissism. Giving oneself over to fashion arises from the wish to be like others (in the absence of a sense of who one is); narcissism involves a wish to be admired by others (in an effort to combat one's sense of worthlessness).

Following this "digression" in which Bion discusses the difficulties inherent in becoming an analyst, he asks the presenter to tell him more about the session:

> Presenter: The patient had the impression that if he remained on duty [as a doctor at the hospital the previous night] he was going to feel ill. He was not feeling ill – he had the impression that this was going to happen.
>
> Bion: In other words, he wasn't going to get cured – he would get these illnesses. It sounds possible that he has never really considered that he has to be very tough indeed to be a doctor at all. In this profession you are always dealing with people at their worst; they are frightened; they are anxious. It is no good taking up that occupation if he is going to end up by being anxious, depressed and frightened too.
>
> (pp. 16–17)

Bion is making an indirect interpretation to the non-psychotic aspect of the presenter's personality. Here, again, the interpretation has a surprisingly pragmatic feel to it: the patient has chosen a career for which he is not emotionally equipped. The patient seems not to be able to face other people's fears without becoming frightened and depressed himself. But, of course, there is more to the interpretation than that. Bion is focusing on a striking contradiction that seems to provide a sense of the nature of the emotional problem for which the patient is seeking help in this session.

Why is the patient presenting the analyst with a contradiction in *this* particular way, at *this* moment? Perhaps the patient did not simply make a poor career choice. Is there something about himself (an aspect of himself that *is* a genuine doctor) from whom the patient feels disconnected? Bion is noticing a communication that is so obvious that it is as invisible as Poe's purloined letter. Perhaps it is this paradox – that the obvious is invisible – that leads Bion's comments to sound odd and concrete. Here, as was the case earlier in the seminar, Bion's observation concerning something that feels "off" to him contains an "imaginative conjecture" (p. 191) regarding the emotional problem that the patient (with the analyst's help) is attempting to "solve" (p. 125) – that is, to think in this session. The question is not simply, "What is leading the patient to feel anxious and fearful?" A more specific problem (or facet of the dynamic tension driving the patient's symptomatology) is alive in the current session. Bion, in his comments that address the patient's choice of profession, seems to be trying out the idea that the patient may feel that *he is not himself.* He chose to try to become a doctor, and yet he feels more drawn to being a passive patient – a person who knows nothing, and wishes to know nothing, about the illness from which he is suffering.

Bion's speculation might be thought of as an interpretation spoken to the non-psychotic aspect of his "imaginary" patient, an aspect of personality that is both unconscious and capable of thinking.

The presenter seems to have been able to make use of this interpretation:

> Presenter: So he left the room to lie down. At this moment he was called to the emergency ward. He went; he worked perfectly. He thought it very curious that he could work well without any difficulty.
>
> (p. 17)

It might be argued that the presenter's account of "what happened next" constitutes a mere recitation of notes that he had written days or weeks earlier. I find this idea unconvincing. The presenter could have said anything in response to Bion's "interpretation": for example, he could have asked a question that would have disrupted analytic thinking in the seminar or he could have made distracting comments about the patient's conscious reasons for seeking medical training. What the presenter does say – "He thought it very curious that he could work well without any difficulty" – involves an unintended, highly meaningful ambiguity. The word *curious* is a euphemism for the patient's feeling at a loss to account for what happened; and at the same time the word *curious* refers to the beginning of the patient's capacity for thinking (the capacity to be curious about what he does not know). The former is a much more passive state of mind than the latter. In his use of the word *curious*, the presenter conveys his growing understanding of the way in which the patient simultaneously wished to think and was afraid to think.

Bion responds by saying, "He goes off to this emergency, and instead of having a heart attack or whatever, he finds that he can be a doctor" (p. 17). The patient, with the analyst's help, is finding that he is able to become a doctor – that is, a person who is able to think and to use that capacity to "dream himself into existence" as a doctor and as an analytic patient. Similarly, with the help of Bion's interpretations, the presenter is able to dream himself into existence as a doctor – that is, as an analyst. He is becoming able to be curious about the patient, a person "at his worst" (a person who is anxious and in dire need of help).

To return to Bion's response to the patient's unexpectedly becoming a genuine doctor, Bion observes,

> Using this [event in which the patient became a doctor] not only for this incident but for many others, you can begin to feel that the patient may after all be a doctor or a potential analyst if, when it comes to a crisis, the doctor emerges. But why in a crisis? If it is really true that he may after all be a doctor, not just by title but the thing itself, why hasn't he discovered that till now? . . . Of course, we believe, as analysts – rightly or wrongly – that analysis is helpful. But that belief is liable to hide from us the extraordinary nature, the mystery of psychoanalysis. Such a lot of analysts seem to be bored with their subject; they have lost the capacity for wonder.
>
> (p. 17)

Two critical elements of Bion's style are audible in these sentences. First, we hear Bion, the doctor, the pragmatist, a person for whom finding "the solution to [the patient's] problem" (p. 100) matters greatly. Bion views his responsibility to be that of helping patients – a rather old-fashioned idea. If we do not believe that analysis is helpful, why are we spending our lives practicing it? How are we to ignore the patient's pain, for it is his pain that leads him to seek help from the analyst? But it does not follow that the analyst's job is to help relieve the patient of pain. Quite the opposite. The analyst's task, for Bion, is to help the patient to live with his pain long enough to do analytic work with it. There is some aspect of the patient that comes to the analyst for analysis. Bion is continually listening for the (often very muted) voice of that part of the patient, and for hints from the patient, concerning what emotional problem this aspect of the patient is trying to think/solve. If the patient is not using the analyst as an analyst (for example, by behaving as if he expects the analyst to be a magician who will turn the patient into the person who he wishes to be), Bion asks himself (and often asks the "dreamt-up" patient) what the patient thinks analysts do. Perhaps second only in frequency to Bion's question, "Why has the patient come for analysis?" is his question, "What does the patient think analysis is?" And he often comments in response to the patient's idea, "That is a very strange conception of analysis." Helping the patient and giving the patient the "correct" (p. 162) analysis (a genuine analytic experience) are, for Bion, one and the same thing.

The second important element of Bion's analytic style that is alive in this passage is his feeling that his awareness of how little he knows is not a source of frustration or disappointment; it is a source of awe and wonderment in the face of the complexity, the beauty, and the horror that constitute human nature. (See Gabbard, 2007, for a discussion of the role of analytic orthodoxy and the use of analytic dogma to evade facing the full complexity and "chaos of the human condition" [p. 35] and of the analytic enterprise.)

In response to the questions and associations that were elicited in Bion by the patient's having begun to develop his capacity for thinking, the presenter continues:

> Later on in the same session he [the patient] asked himself this question [How did he manage to genuinely become a doctor?] and said, "If I had known that analysis could do this for me I wouldn't have waited for a crisis before coming."
>
> (p. 17)

The reader can hear in this comment a shift in the balance of power between the patient as an assailant of his own capacity for thinking and the patient as a thinking doctor. The doctor is now able to face the fact that he is ill while remaining alive to his feelings; he is able to make use of his awareness of his emotions to give direction to his thinking; and he is able to use his thinking to become "an analyst" who actively takes responsibility for his role in his own analysis.

Bion recognizes that the satisfaction to be taken by the patient in this achievement is balanced by feelings of sadness that are equally intense: "One of the peculiarities of progress is that it always makes you feel depressed or regretful that you didn't discover it sooner" (p. 17). This interpretation is meant not only for the imaginary patient being dreamt up in the seminar, but also for the presenter who, I think, Bion feels is regretful that it has taken him so long to become an analyst for his patient. Perhaps the presenter recognized in the course of the seminar that he had relied for a long time on the thinking of others – the "training analyst" in himself – who had been afraid to respond freshly, without preconception, to what he was perceiving and feeling in the analytic sessions. In other words, to this point, he had been unable to invent/rediscover psychoanalysis with this patient.

Still another element of Bion's analytic style can be felt in this portion of the seminar. As we have seen, Bion is continually aware of the way in which each patient in each analytic hour unconsciously feels that his life is at stake (and, it seems to me, that Bion believes that, in an important sense, the patient is correct in believing so). After all, to the extent that a patient cannot think, he cannot be alive to his experience. But Bion, here, takes a more radical position than he took earlier regarding the analyst's use of himself in his effort to help the patient. What he adds is critical to who Bion is as an analyst:

> You are an analyst, or a father or a mother, because you believe you are capable of the affection or understanding which is so necessary but which is felt [by the patient and the child] to be so unimportant [i.e. it is invisible to them because it is completely taken for granted, as it should be] . . . It is liable to be lost sight of that what we, as doctors and psycho-analysts, are concerned with is helping human beings . . . We may have to upset them in the course of the analysis, but that is not what we are trying to do. With this patient it may be very important to show him, when the time comes, that there exists [in the analyst] some capacity for affection, sympathy, understanding – not just diagnoses [interpretations] and surgery, not just analytic jargon, but interest in the person. You can't make doctors or analysts – they have to be born.
>
> (p. 18)

Bion, in his characteristically understated way, is saying that, for him, being an analyst involves more than understanding the patient and communicating to him that understanding in a form that he can make use of; being an analyst involves, at times, feeling *and showing* one's affection for the patient about whom the analyst cares deeply. This is something that one cannot be taught to do; one must be born with a capacity to do it and a wish to do it.

### 3. *A man who was perpetually awake (São Paulo, 1978, Seminar No. 1)*

In this seminar, the patient being presented is a 38-year-old economist who has a rather mechanical walk and conducts himself in a stiff manner, for example, by opening a session by saying, "Very well, Doctor," or "I have brought you some dreams today" (p. 141).

Bion very soon asks another of his "odd" questions: "Why does he say they are dreams?" (p. 142). Bion is immediately cutting to the core of what he believes to be the emotional problem with which the patient is unconsciously asking for help from the analyst: the non-psychotic aspect of the patient recognizes that the psychotic aspect of himself is dominating his personality and consequently he cannot dream. Bion is suggesting with his question that, to the extent that the patient is psychotic, he cannot differentiate dreaming from waking perception – that is, he cannot tell whether he is asleep or awake. For Bion (1962a), the psychotic patient (or aspect of the patient) is unable to generate and maintain a barrier (the "contact-barrier," p. 21) between conscious and unconscious aspects of mind. In the absence of differentiation between conscious and unconscious mental experience, the individual "cannot go to sleep and cannot wake up" (p. 7). He lives in a world in which internally generated perception (hallucination) is undifferentiable both from perception of external events and from dreaming. Consequently, the patient, in an effort to protect himself from this frightening awareness, pretends to be a person who is interested in dreams.

The presenter, like the reader, has not thought to ask himself why the patient says he had dreams, what the patient means when he speaks of having had dreams, and whether or not the patient, at this moment, knows what a dream is. Nonplussed by Bion's question, "Why does he say they are dreams?" the presenter replies, "He simply tells me so" (p. 142).

The element of Bion's analytic style to which I am drawing attention here is his extraordinarily quick wit. Here, he is casting the presenter as a straight man in a magic show in which Bion pulls a rabbit out of the presenter's vest pocket. Bion is perfectly straight-faced throughout. Wit is neither an inherently good nor bad quality of character. How it is used is what matters. At 80, Bion, in this instance, is playing the role of enigmatic, idiosyncratic, unpredictable, razor-sharp, old man – a role that seems to suit him. Another example of Bion's wit that comes to mind is a comment that he made in

Brasilia Seminar No. 8. The presenter told Bion that the patient had said that he had managed to control his envy, but the patient kept moving anxiously on the couch throughout the session. Bion replied, "He controlled envy and his envy is extremely annoyed about it" (1987, p. 48).

It is never easy (perhaps impossible) to "read" Bion (i.e. to say with certainty who he "really is" at a given moment). He is a thoughtful, earnest teacher, fully aware of the limits of his knowledge and of his personality and, at the same time, a man who means what he says and a man who invites (and helps) students and patients to do the same. There is also a reticence to Bion in the "Clinical Seminars." His wit and his penchant for enigmatic statements are parts, I believe, of an effort to safeguard the sanctity of his privacy. This, too, is an integral part of Bion's analytic style, an integral part of who Bion is as an analyst and as a person.

A few moments later in the seminar, Bion speaks at greater length about the question that the patient was raising in Bion's mind:

> So why does the patient come to see a psycho-analyst and say he had a dream? I can imagine myself saying to a patient, "Where were you last night? What did you see?" If the patient told me he didn't see anything – he just went to bed – I would say, "Well, I still want to know where you went and what you saw."
>
> (p. 142)

Bion, in this way, is saying to the non-psychotic part of the patient's personality that he understands that the patient does not know when he is awake and when he is asleep. So when the patient tells him that he went to bed, Bion treats the "dream" as an experience that has all the qualities of waking life experience. Bion continues: "If the patient said, 'Ah, well, I had a dream', then I would want to know why he says it was a dream" (p. 142). By not accepting the patient's use of the word "dream" (which serves to evade the truth), Bion is helping the non-psychotic aspect of the patient's personality to think (which involves facing the reality of the current hegemony of the psychotic aspect of his personality). Bion is implicitly stating his belief that such recognition of the truth of what is occurring influences the balance of power between the psychotic and the non-psychotic aspects of the personality.

Bion, a little later on, elaborates on this idea: "when he says that [he had a dream], he is awake and "conscious," as we call it" (p. 142). In other words, what the patient is calling *dreams*, we would call *hallucinations*. The patient cannot differentiate visual events that he has while sleeping from visual perceptions he has when he is "awake." Bion adds, "He is inviting you and himself to be prejudiced in favour of a state of mind in which we are when awake" (p. 142) – that is, he is trying to convince the analyst that there is only one state – that of being awake – so that both patient and analyst can agree that the patient is not psychotic and is simply reporting what he perceives in a waking state. The patient is insisting that because there is only one state – that of wakefulness – there is no difference between perception and hallucination, dream-life and waking life; consequently, there is no such thing as psychosis.

The element of Bion's analytic style with which I am concerned here is the absolute directness with which he speaks to the (dreamt-up) patient. He senses almost immediately when the patient is using words in a way that involves a slippage of meaning that prevents painful recognition of the truth. Bion, as in the instance under discussion, then speaks to the patient in a way that restores the proper meaning to words, which in turn allows for thinking and "ordinary human intercourse" (p. 197) to begin or resume. To be able consistently to hear and respond to such slippages of meaning requires a very fine ear indeed.

## Concluding comments

It is impossible to give an adequate rendering of an analyst's style since his style is informed by nothing less than everything that he is as a person and as an analyst. Though I greatly admire many of the qualities of Bion's analytic style that are brought to life in the "Clinical Seminars," I do not view his style as a model to emulate. Rather, as Bion states in the seminars, "The way I do psychoanalysis is of no importance to anybody excepting myself, but it may give you some idea of how *you* do analysis, and that *is* important" (p. 224).

# 6

# Bion's four principles of mental functioning

Bion's life-work as a psychoanalytic theorist was the formulation of a theory of thinking. Over a span of four decades, virtually every one of Bion's papers, books, lectures, clinical seminars, and notes to himself (his "cogitations") involves an effort to develop one aspect or another of that theory of thinking. Bion experimented with a variety of metaphors (models) in his effort to capture the nature of thinking and its consequences. The major metaphors with which he experimented include the idea of the interplay of the work group and the basic assumption groups; an intersubjective conception of projective identification; the theory of alpha-function; the concept of the container-contained; the theory of L, H, and K linkages and of attacks on linking; the concept of binocular vision; the grid; psychic transformations; and the concept of "O."

With a body of work as extensive as Bion's, I find it useful to state in as few words as possible what I discern to be the fundamental tenets running through that work. Bion (1962a), in the same spirit, commented, "Psycho-analytic virtue lies not in the number of theories the analyst can command but the minimum number with which he can meet any contingency he is likely to meet" (p. 88). Accordingly, I will begin by stating in a highly condensed fashion what I think of as "the four principles of mental functioning" that I believe constitute the core of Bion's theory of thinking. My ideas are offered as points of departure for thoughts about Bion's theory of thinking, not as end points.

After presenting, in the space of a single paragraph, my conception of Bion's four principles of mental functioning, I will go on to discuss at greater length each of the principles that I have proposed. Finally, I will look closely at one of Bion's clinical seminars in an effort to demonstrate something of the way in which his clinical thinking is informed by his theory of thinking.

## Bion's theory of thinking

*Bion's theory of thinking is built upon four overlapping and interconnecting principles of mental functioning: (1) thinking is driven by the human need to know the truth – the reality of who one is and what is occurring in one's life; (2) it requires two minds to think a person's most disturbing thoughts; (3) the capacity for thinking is developed in order to come to terms with thoughts derived from one's disturbing emotional experience; and (4) there is an inherent psychoanalytic function of the personality, and dreaming is the principal process through which that function is performed.*

### *1. The human need to know the truth*

Organizing Bion's theory of thinking into four principles of mental functioning is my own device, not Bion's. So far as I am aware, Bion never used the term *principle of mental functioning* in connection with his own work on thinking. Freud's (1911) "Formulations on the Two Principles of Mental Functioning" addresses the way in which psychological development involves the movement from the dominance of the pleasure principle to the dominance of the reality principle. Freud believed that in conceiving of psychological development in this way he was "bringing the psychological significance of the real external world into the structure of our theories" (p. 218). As will be seen, each of Bion's four principles of mental functioning is similarly addressed most fundamentally to the individual's relationship to reality. But Bion's conception of the relationship between reality and thinking is quite different from Freud's. Freud's two principles begin with the search for pleasure in the discharge of instinctual tension (the pleasure principle) and end with the perception of, and the capacity to adapt to, reality (the reality principle). Each of Bion's four principles begins not with instinctual pressure, but with lived emotional experience in the real world, and ends with thinking and feeling that experience. Moreover, Bion's understanding of unconscious thinking differs markedly from Freud's idea, in that, for Freud (1911), the unconscious is characterized by an "entire disregard for reality-testing" (p. 225), while, for Bion (1967), ". . . without [unconscious] phantasies and without dreams you have not the means with which to think out your problems" (p. 25).

In formulating the first of Bion's four principles of mental functioning, I will draw heavily on Bion's earliest contribution to psychoanalysis, *Experiences in Groups and Other Papers* (1959). (Though *Experiences in Groups* was published in 1959, the papers included in it were published much earlier: a "Pre-view" [written in collaboration with John Rickman] was published in 1943; "Experiences in Groups" is a set of seven essays that were originally published between 1948 and 1951; and "Group Dynamics: A Review" was first published in 1952. For the sake of brevity, I will refer to *Experiences in Groups and Other Papers* simply as *Experiences in Groups*.) In that collection of papers, Bion introduces a radical reformulation of the psychoanalytic conception of thinking and its psychopathology. What Borges said of his first book of poetry, *Fervor de Buenos Aires* (1923), might be said of Bion's *Experiences in Groups*: "I feel that all my subsequent writing has only developed themes first taken up there; I feel that all during my lifetime I have been re-writing that one book" (Borges, 1970b, p. 225).

Although I have read *Experiences in Groups* many times over the decades, I have recently "rediscovered" this collection of papers. As a result, the metaphors for thinking that Bion develops in *Experiences in Groups* hold a particular freshness for me now, which I hope will vitalize my attempts to articulate the essential tenets of Bion's theory of thinking. (When Bion speaks of thinking, he is always referring to thinking and feeling, which he views as inseparable aspects of a single psychological event.)

*Experiences in Groups* (1959) is at its core a study of the relationship between that aspect of "group mentality" (p. 60) that is able to think ("the work group," p. 98) and that aspect of group mentality that is unable to think (the "basic assumption groups," p. 153). The ideas that Bion develops concerning thinking in groups constitute the foundation of a general theory of thinking. Bion states that he views the psychoanalytic dyad as a small group: "The psycho-analytical situation is not 'individual psychology' but 'pair' [psychology]" (p. 131). Moreover, implicit in Bion's thinking about groups is the idea that the individual psyche might be thought of as a group comprised of different parts of the personality. That intrapsychic "group" engages in conversations between aspects of the personality that are able to think and other aspects of the personality that hate and fear thinking. (Bion, 1957, later develops the idea of intrapsychic conversations between parts of the personality in "Differentiation of the Psychotic from the Non-Psychotic Personalities.")

Throughout "Experiences in Groups" (1948–1951) – the series of papers that forms the core of *Experiences in Groups* – Bion eschews psychoanalytic terminology and, instead, invents his own everyday language for discussing the group experiences that he has observed and in which he has participated. For example, Bion does not use the term *phantasy* to refer to the shared unconscious beliefs of a group and instead invents his own more expressive term, *basic assumption*. The "basic assumptions" are the fearful orientations to reality that shape group experience so profoundly that it is inadequate to think of them as mere ideas. They are so basic as to warrant the term *proto-mental* – thinking "in which physical and mental activity is undifferentiated" (Bion, 1959, p. 154).

Bion describes three types of basic assumption groups – three forms of group mentality that groups generate in an effort to evade thinking: the dependent, the pairing, and the fight–flight basic assumption groups. To evade thinking is to evade the task of coming to terms with, and making efforts to modify, what is actually occurring both within and outside the group. The "dependent" basic assumption group is based on a shared assumption that the group leader will "solve all their [the group's] problems" (p. 82). At the same time, the group adopts an "unshakeable indifference to everything I [the group leader] say" (p. 83). The group members' indifference to the leader's ideas derives from the fact that the members are not the least bit interested in making use of what the leader says for the purpose of thinking for themselves. Quite the contrary, the group opposes thinking and insists on simply waiting for the leader to magically set things right. Thinking and making use of one's thoughts to try to effect changes in the real world are the leader's responsibilities, not theirs. Interpretations are more likely to be met by "awe than a pause for thought" (p. 85).

The "pairing" basic assumption group is based on a jointly held assumption that two members of the group will produce "a Messiah, be it a person, idea or Utopia" (p. 152) who (or which) will rescue the group from their feelings of destructiveness, hatred, and despair. Again, the group members steadfastly oppose doing any psychological work of their own and, instead, wait to be saved.

The "fight–flight" (p. 153) basic assumption group holds the proto-mental and unconscious belief that all of the group's problems can be solved by means of fighting or taking flight from an enemy. Neither fighting nor fleeing requires any thinking on the part of the group. Thus, for all three types of basic assumption groups, genuine thinking is replaced by magical thinking. This allows the group, at least temporarily, to evade reality rather than attempt to think about it and modify it.

The basic assumption groups reflect the group's "hatred of learning by experience" (p. 86) as well as its "hatred of a process of development" (p. 89). These fears and hatreds are born of the group members' fears of emotional experience "for which they do not feel prepared" (p. 82). In other words, the basic assumption group mentalities are founded on the wish to be able to arrive "fully equipped as an adult fitted by instinct to know without training [i.e. without having to learn from experience] or development exactly how to live and move" (p. 89) as a mature adult. The group fears and hates the fact that immaturity is an inescapable part of the human condition and that the processes of learning and maturing require that one tolerate feelings of not knowing, of confusion, and of powerlessness.

And yet, despite the fact that we are powerfully drawn to magical solutions (forms of non-thinking), for Bion, groups (and individuals) are at their core "hopelessly committed to a developmental procedure" (p. 89) – that is, to thinking, learning from experience, and growing up. This commitment reflects what Bion believes to be a need that is perhaps the most powerful of all human strivings: the need for truth.

> It is almost as if human beings were aware of the painful and often fatal consequences of having to act without an adequate grasp of reality, and therefore were aware of the need for truth as a criterion in the evaluation of their findings [perceptions].
>
> (1959, p. 100)

> . . . a sense of reality matters to the individual in the way that food, drink, air and excretion of waste products matter.
>
> (1962a, p. 42)

In other words, thinking that lacks an "adequate grasp of reality," an adequate sense of the truth (for example, each of the various forms of magical thinking employed by the basic assumption groups), is useless in one's effort to learn from experience and to grow psychologically. Magical ideas cannot be linked with other ideas in the process of generating a line of thought that one can use to solve emotional problems that arise in the course of a life lived in the real world. One cannot construct a line of rational thought on a foundation of ideas generated for the purpose of evading the truth. Instead, the individual or group remains in a solipsistic world of magical thinking – "thinking" that is based on the idea/wish that one creates the world as one goes. A magical world is simultaneously an ideal place and a nightmare: one cannot learn or grow; one is damned to live in an eternal, static, directionless present. Bion interpreted a patient's fearful use of magical thinking by saying, "What a shame it is that you have been reduced to omnipotence" (Grotstein, 2003, personal communication).

The human need for truth leads us ultimately to loosen our reliance on the illusion or delusion of safety that is provided by magical thinking, and to attempt to engage in genuine thinking – thinking that confronts reality in its full, unforgiving alterity. Only by means of such a confrontation with the truth in the act of thinking is it possible to do something with (to learn from and efficaciously attempt to modify) the reality of one's lived emotional experience. For Bion, *the human need to know the truth of one's experience is the most fundamental impetus for thinking*. This conception of thinking constitutes the first and most fundamental of what I am calling Bion's four principles of mental functioning.

Closely tied to Bion's first principle of mental functioning are three ideas that are critical to Bion's theory of thinking. The first of these is the idea that non-thinking (i.e. evasion of thinking) and genuine thinking are inseparable and, in fact, depend upon one another. For example, the thinking performed by the work group (the group mentality in which genuine thinking may take place), on the one hand, and the various forms of magical thinking that characterize the basic assumption groups, on the other, constitute two facets of a single experience. Primitive fears of learning by experience and of emotional development are the very experiences from which a group learns about itself and develops. In the absence of the painful psychic reality constituted by these primitive fears, we would have nothing to think about and nothing to learn from: no "therapy could result unless these psychotic patterns [the basic assumptions] were laid bare [regardless of how psychologically healthy the members of a group may be]" (p. 181). The essence of "developmental conflict" (p. 128) from which the group grows is "the painful bringing together" (p. 128) of the reality of the primitive (the "psychotic" basic assumption beliefs, fears, and hatreds) and the "sophisticated" (p. 128) (the capacity for genuine thinking). In other words, mature thinking is generated in response to our most archaic fears.

The second of Bion's ideas, which is closely associated with his first principle of mental functioning, is the notion that genuine thinking requires a tolerance for not knowing, a tolerance for "being in uncertainties, mysteries, doubts, without any irritable reaching after fact and reason" (Keats, 1817; quoted by Bion, 1970, p. 125). Genuine thinking, though driven by the need to know what is true, is at the same time characterized by a firm recognition that conclusions are always inconclusive, endings are always beginnings: "Every emotional experience of knowledge gained is at the same time an emotional experience of ignorance unilluminated" (Bion, 1992, p. 275). This aspect of Bion's theory of thinking culminated in his concept of "O" (1970, p. 26) – the unknowable, inexpressible truth of one's experience (see Ogden, 2004b, for a discussion of the concept of "O" and its clinical implications).

The concept of "binocular vision" (1962a, p. 86) – "the need for employing a technique of constantly changing points of view" (1959, p. 86) – is the third of Bion's ideas that I view as a "corollary" to his first principle of mental functioning. This concept holds that thinking necessarily involves viewing reality from multiple vantage points (or "vertices" [Bion, 1970, p. 83]) simultaneously – for example, from the points of view of the conscious and the unconscious mind; the autistic-contiguous (Ogden, 1987, 1989b, c), the paranoid-schizoid, and the depressive positions; the work group and the basic assumption groups; the psychotic and the non-psychotic parts of the personality; and so on. Reality viewed from a single vantage point represents a failure to think. This can be seen in clearly pathological circumstances such as hallucinations, delusions, perversions, and mania, as well as in states that superficially do not appear pathological – for example, instances of strident pacifism or rigid adherence to the views of a school of psychoanalytic thought. Viewing reality from multiple vantage points allows each vertex (each way of viewing reality) to enter into a mutually mutative conversation with other ways of seeing/knowing/experiencing.

This idea of multiple vertices lies at the very heart of Bion's conception of sanity and insanity. If one has only one way of viewing reality, one cannot think, one is psychotic. Sanity involves a capacity for generating and maintaining a multiplicity of perspectives from which to view/experience one's life in the real world (including the reality of one's own personality). For example, a medical student in a state of relative psychological health may be able simultaneously to experience the cadaver that he is dissecting as the body of a once-living human being; a non-human object constructed for the purpose of teaching anatomy; terrifying, inescapable evidence of the reality of death (his own death, the death of those he loves, the death of the patients he will treat); a reflection of the generosity of the person who granted permission for the use of his or her remains for purposes of medical education; and the scene of a rape born of the medical student's unconscious belief that his violent entry into the body of the cadaver is tantamount to rape, and, at an even deeper level, his feeling raped by the cadaver (in the form of the cadaver forcefully entering his psyche as the formaldehyde enters his body, leaving its color and odor on him and in him). Thinking, so conceived, is a process in which ideas and feelings live in continual conversation with one another, a conversation in which thoughts are forever in the process of being transformed (de-integrated) and formed anew as a consequence of shifting organizations of meaning.

## 2. *It takes two minds to think one's disturbing thoughts*

Bion (1959) introduced what I am calling his *second principle of mental functioning* in the course of discussing the relationship between the group leader and the group. As mentioned earlier, the analyst leading the group is as subject to the draw of basic assumption "thinking" as are the other members of the group. This is not a reflection of the analyst's psychopathology, inexperience, or ineptitude; rather, the analyst's participation in the basic assumption groups is indispensable to his attempt to understand what is true to what is occurring in the group:

> . . . many interpretations, and amongst them the most important, have to be made on the strength of the analyst's own emotional reactions . . . The analyst feels he is being manipulated so as to be

> playing a part, no matter how difficult to recognize, in somebody else's phantasy . . . [The analyst has] a sense of experiencing strong feelings and at the same time a belief that their existence is quite adequately justified by the objective situation [i.e. he believes that his feelings are a reasonable response to what is occurring in the group].
>
> (1959, p. 149)

Bion, in this passage, is articulating for the first time the clinical basis for his radical revision of Klein's (1946) concept of projective identification (see Ogden, 1979, 1982). Klein insisted that projective identification is strictly an intrapsychic phenomenon. Nevertheless, the language she used to describe projective identification suggests an interpersonal dimension: "Split-off parts of the ego are . . . projected on to the mother or, as I would rather call it, *into* the mother" (Klein, 1946, p. 8, italics in original). In Bion's psychological-interpersonal version of projective identification, the analyst must be able to experience himself in accord with the feelings elicited in him by the real interpersonal pressure that accompanies "somebody else's phantasy"; yet, it is critical that the analyst at the same time be able

> to shake [him]self out of the numbing feeling of reality that is a concomitant of this state [which ability] is the prime requisite of the analyst in the group: if he can do this he is in a position to give what I believe is the correct interpretation, and thereby to see its connection with the previous interpretation, the validity of which he has been caused to doubt.
>
> (Bion, 1959, pp. 149–150)

In other words, when in the grip of projective identification, the analyst loses touch with the logic of his previous thoughts because his capacity to think has been compromised ("numbed"). He has unwittingly participated, for example, in the evasion of reality (the non-thinking or anti-thinking) that is occurring in a group. In shaking himself out of the psychic reality engendered in him, the analyst is not "regaining" his earlier capacity to think. Rather, having been changed by the experience of participating in the particular paralysis of, or attack on, thinking that characterized the specific intersubjective state (the basic assumption) of the group, the analyst is now in a new position (i.e. he has developed a new vertex) from which to understand what is occurring. Based on that new understanding, he may be able to communicate to the group something of what he believes to be the nature of the fears and hatreds that the group is experiencing. The aim of the analyst in putting such thoughts into words is not to solve the emotional problems of the group; rather, he offers interpretations in an effort to help the group do the work of thinking the truth (the reality) of the emotional experience that is unfolding.

A decade later, in "A Theory of Thinking" (1962b) and *Learning from Experience* (1962a), Bion fleshes out his conception of thinking as an intersubjective experience:

> Ordinarily the personality of the infant, like other elements of the environment [such as the provision of holding, feeding, and loving], is managed by the mother. If mother and child are adjusted to each other projective identification plays a role in the management [of the infant's personality] through the operation of a rudimentary and fragile reality sense.
>
> (Bion, 1962b, p. 114)

Thus, in the process of healthy projective identification, mother and infant think together and, in so doing, the infant achieves "a rudimentary and fragile reality sense," a rudimentary capacity to perceive himself, his mother, and the world realistically.

Bion continues:

> As a realistic activity [i.e. an actual interaction involving two people] it [the infant's contribution to the projective identification] shows itself as behaviour reasonably calculated to arouse in the mother feelings of which the infant wishes to be rid. If the infant feels it is dying [i.e. feels as if he is losing his rudimentary sense of self as a consequence of his inability to cope with his disturbing emotional experience] it can arouse fears that it is dying in the mother. A well-balanced mother can accept these and respond therapeutically: that is to say in a manner that makes the infant feel it is receiving its frightened personality [no longer dissolving or fragmenting] back again but in a form that it can tolerate – the fears are manageable by the infant personality.
>
> (Bion, 1962b, pp. 114–115)

In this way, mother and infant together think thoughts that had previously been so disturbing as to be unthinkable by the infant on his own: "The activity we know as 'thinking' was in origin . . . projective identification" (Bion, 1962a, p. 31).

In reconceptualizing projective identification in this way, Bion is expressing what I view as his second principle of mental functioning: *it requires two minds to think one's most disturbing thoughts*. The two minds engaged in thinking may be those of the mother and infant, the group leader and group member, the patient and analyst, the supervisor and supervisee, the husband and wife, and so on. The two minds may also be two "parts" of the personality: the psychotic and non-psychotic parts of the personality (Bion, 1957); "the dreamer who dreams the dream" and "the dreamer who understands the dream" (Grotstein, 2000); the "dream-work" and the "understanding-work" (Sandler, 1976, p. 40); and so forth. When the thinking capacity of the parts of the personality in conversation with one another proves inadequate to the task of thinking one's troubling experience, the minds of two separate people are required for thinking one's previously unthinkable thoughts.

Since every stage of development involves facing emotional experience for which one feels unprepared, we are throughout our lives in need of other people with whom to think. As Bion (1987) puts it, "the human unit is a couple; it takes two human beings to make one" (p. 222). Winnicott (1960) famously puts it in his own way: "There is no such thing as an infant" [apart from the mother] (p. 39fn).

## 3. *Thinking develops in order to cope with thoughts*

Bion introduced in "A Theory of Thinking" (1962b) and developed in *Learning from Experience* (1962a) what I view as his third principle of mental functioning: "*Thinking is a development forced on the psyche by the pressure of thoughts and not the other way round*" (1962b, p. 111, italics added). This is a theory that "differs from any theory . . . [that views] thought as a product of thinking" (p. 111).

In earliest post-natal life, all experience – even what we later view as soothing experience – is disturbing in that it is utterly new and unexpected. For example, air as a medium in which to live has no equivalent in intrauterine life. And breast-feeding, for which the infant is instinctually "hard wired," almost always proves to be difficult at first. The breast for which the infant has a "pre-conception" (Bion, 1962b, p. 111) is not the real breast that the infant encounters (even when the mother is highly sensitive to the infant's psychosomatic state). The infant's (metaphorical) first thought is not of the breast, but of the "no-breast" (1962b, p. 112) – the absent breast or that part of the experience of the actual breast that differs (beyond tolerable limits) from the pre-conceived breast: "If [the infant's] capacity for toleration of frustration [with the help of the mother] is sufficient the 'no-breast' [experience] inside becomes a thought and an apparatus for 'thinking' it develops" (p. 112). Alternatively, if the infant is unable to tolerate the tension and psychic pain associated with frustration (even with the mother's help), the experience of the "no-breast" is short-circuited. What might have become a thought becomes either an evacuation of tension (for example, in the form of action or excessive projective identification) or an evasion of thinking (for example, in the form of omnipotent "thinking"). What might have become an apparatus for thinking a thought becomes an "hypertrophic . . . apparatus of projective identification" (p. 112).

Bion's theory of alpha-function is an elaboration of the third principle of mental functioning – the idea that thoughts give rise to thinking. Bion posits that the individual's encounters with reality generate "beta-elements," "sense-impressions related to an emotional experience" (1962a, p. 17). These sense impressions (in the absence of further transformation) cannot be linked in the process of thinking and are fit only for evacuation – for example, by means of projective identification. But we must not lose sight of the fact that beta-elements constitute our sole psychological connection with reality. Beta-elements might be thought of as "those unthoughtlike thoughts that are the souls of thought" (Poe, 1848, p. 80). Bion hypothesizes that "alpha-function" (1962a, p. 6) (an as-yet-unknown, and probably unknowable, set of mental operations) serves to transform beta-elements into alpha-elements that can be linked to form dream-thoughts. Dream-thoughts are the symbolic representation of the disturbing experience that was originally registered primarily in sensory terms (i.e. as beta-elements). The capacities for alpha-function, dreaming, thinking, and remembering are "called into existence to cope with thoughts" (1962b, p. 111).

In addition to the theory of alpha-function, a second important line of Bion's thinking, the concept of the "container-contained" (1962a, 1970; see also Ogden, 2004c), represents an extension of Bion's third principle of mental functioning. The third principle – the idea that thinking develops in order to cope with thoughts – is in essence a conception of the way mental functioning inherently involves a forceful dynamic interplay between thoughts and the capacity for thinking. The "container" (1962a, p. 90), in Bion's theory of the container-contained, is not a thing but a process: it is the unconscious psychological work of dreaming, operating in concert with preconscious dream-like thinking (reverie) and conscious secondary process thinking. The term *contained* (p. 90) refers to thoughts and feelings that are in the process of being derived from one's lived emotional experience.

When the relationship between container and contained is a healthy one, growth occurs in both and is reflected in the enhancement of the individual's capacity for "tolerated doubt" (p. 92). So far as the container is concerned, there is an expansion of the capacity for doing unconscious psychological work (i.e. dreaming one's lived experience). The growth of the contained is reflected in an enrichment of the range and depth of thoughts that one is able to derive from one's lived experience in the world.

Under pathological conditions, the container may become destructive to the contained, resulting in a limitation of what one is able to "retain [of one's] . . . knowledge and experience" (1962a, p. 93). What one has learned from experience is no longer available to oneself; one feels as if important parts of oneself are missing. Conversely, the contained may overwhelm and destroy the container – for example, in nightmares, when the dream-thought becomes so disturbing as to overwhelm the capacity for dreaming, and, as a result, the dreamer wakes up in a state of fright. Similarly, in children's play disruptions, the thought being "worked on" in play (the contained) overwhelms the container (the capacity for playing). (For further discussion of the concept of the container-contained and its relationship to Winnicott's concept of holding, see Ogden, 2004c.)

Viewing thoughts as the impetus for thinking leads the analyst in the clinical setting to be continually asking himself what disturbing (unthinkable) thought the patient at any given moment in the analysis is asking the analyst to help him to think. The analyst is also aware that even as the patient is asking for help in thinking, the patient fears and hates the analyst for attempting to do just that: "Patients hate having feelings at all . . ." (Bion, 1987, p. 183).

The idea that the development of an apparatus for thinking takes place as a response to disturbing thoughts also contributes to a theory of the therapeutic process: the analyst's being receptive to, and doing psychological work with, the patient's unthinkable thoughts serves not as a substitute or replacement for the patient's capacity for thinking, but as an experience of *thinking with the patient* in a way that serves to create conditions in which the patient may be able to further develop his own inborn rudimentary capacity for thinking (his own inborn capacity for alpha-function).

Thus, the goal of the psychoanalytic process is not that of helping the patient resolve unconscious intrapsychic conflict (or any other emotional problem); rather, the aim of psychoanalysis is to help the patient develop his own capacity for thinking and feeling his experience. Once that process is under way, the patient is in a position to begin to confront and come to terms with his own emotional problems. The patient is increasingly able to think with people other than the analyst and to engage in kinds of "conversations" with them and with himself that involve different aspects of his own personality that previously had not been available to him for the purpose of conscious, preconscious, and unconscious psychological work.

### *4. Dreaming and the psychoanalytic function of the personality*

The fourth of what I think of as Bion's principles of mental functioning is the idea that *there exists an inherent psychoanalytic function of the personality, and dreaming is the principal process for performing that function.*

In positing "a psycho-analytic function of personality" (1962a, p. 89), Bion is proposing that the human personality is constitutionally equipped with mental operations that generate personal symbolic meaning, consciousness, and the potential for unconscious psychological work with one's emotional problems. All three of these components of the psychoanalytic function of the mind mediate psychological growth. What makes this function of the personality "psycho-analytic" is the fact that the psychological work is achieved to a large extent by means of viewing an emotional situation simultaneously from the perspective of the conscious and unconscious mind. For Bion, dreaming (which is synonymous with unconscious thinking) is the principal psychological form in which this work is performed.

Dreaming occurs continuously both while we are awake and while we are asleep (Bion, 1962a). Just as the stars remain in the sky even when their light is obscured by the glare of the sun, so, too, dreaming is a continuous function of the mind that persists even when our dreams are obscured from consciousness by the glare of waking life. Dreaming is the most free, most inclusive, and most deeply penetrating form of psychological work of which human beings are capable. In conceiving of the psychoanalytic function of the personality in this way, Bion is radically revising Freud's understanding of the work of dreaming and of the analytic process. For Freud, the goal of dreaming and of psychoanalysis is that of making the unconscious conscious – that is, making derivatives of unconscious experience available to conscious (secondary process) thinking.

In contrast, for Bion, the unconscious is the seat of the psychoanalytic function of the personality, and, consequently, in order to do psychoanalytic work, one must make the conscious unconscious – that is, make conscious lived experience available to the unconscious work of dreaming. The work of dreaming, for Bion, is the psychological work by means of which we create personal, symbolic meaning thereby becoming ourselves. In other words, we dream ourselves into existence. In the absence of the capacity for dreaming, we are unable to create meaning that feels personal to us: we cannot differentiate between hallucination and perception, between our own perceptions and those of others, and between our dream-life and our waking life. In this psychological state, one "cannot go to sleep and cannot wake up . . . the psychotic patient behaves as if he were in precisely this state" (Bion, 1962a, p. 7).

Moreover, from Bion's perspective, dreaming is the psychological activity through which we achieve consciousness. Dreaming "makes a barrier against [unconscious] mental phenomena which might overwhelm the patient's awareness [for example] that he is talking to a friend, and, at the same time, makes it impossible for [conscious] awareness that he is talking to a friend to overwhelm his [unconscious] phantasies" (Bion, 1962a, p. 15). Dreaming is not a product of the differentiation of the conscious and unconscious mind; it is the dreaming that creates and maintains that differentiation, and, in so doing, generates human consciousness.

In sum, Bion's fourth principle of mental functioning holds that dreaming constitutes the central component of the psychoanalytic function of the personality. Dreaming is our profoundest form of thinking and constitutes the principal medium through which we achieve human consciousness, psychological growth, and the capacity to create personal, symbolic meaning from our lived experience.

I will end this section by returning to its beginning. *I view Bion's theory of thinking as a theory built upon four fundamental principles of mental functioning: (1) the impetus for all thinking is the human need to know the truth – the reality of who one is and what is occurring in one's life; (2) it takes two minds to think one's most disturbing thoughts; (3) the capacity for thinking develops in order to come to terms with thoughts derived from one's disturbing emotional experience; and (4) there is an inherent psychoanalytic function of the personality, and dreaming is the principal process through which that function is performed.*

## Bion's clinical thinking

I will now offer an illustration of the way in which Bion's clinical thinking is informed by his theory of thinking and the four principles of mental functioning that I believe underlie that theory. The clinical work that I will discuss is taken from the sixteenth of the clinical seminars that Bion conducted in São Paolo in 1978 (Bion, 1987, pp. 200–202).

The seminar begins:

> Presenter: The patient lay down on the couch and started to talk. "Mrs J is the owner of the house where I live. She is eighty-eight years old. I dreamt that she was walking along the road, talking about the rental agreement." Then she started shouting, "What are you doing there behind me? Tell me *immediately*. You are a dishonest liar!" This took me by surprise.
>
> (p. 200)

This opening paragraph is confusing to me each time I read it. The pronoun *she* is ambiguous in the phrase, "Then she started shouting . . ." Is the presenter using the pronoun *she* to continue telling the dream in the patient's words, in which case "she" (who is shouting) refers to a figure in the dream? Or has the presenter begun to tell the dream to Bion in his own words, in which case "she" is the patient, and the sentences in quotation marks that follow are the words that the patient shouted at the presenter: "What are you doing there behind me? Tell me *immediately*. You are a dishonest liar!" It is impossible for Bion (who is listening to the presentation, not reading it) to know whether Mrs J in the dream is shouting at the patient or whether the patient in waking life is shouting at the presenter. Each time I read this passage, it is only after taking pains to figure out what the quotation marks are indicating that I am able to determine that the patient is interrupting her own telling of her dream to shout at the analyst. The analyst remarks to Bion, "This took me by surprise." This took me by surprise, too, because of the way the presenter is making it difficult for the reader, and impossible for Bion, to know what is dream-life and what is waking life.

Bion responds:

> I wonder what the difficulty is. If she knows that you are a dishonest liar, then obviously you would be telling lies behind her back. At the same time, why ask you what you are doing behind her back? Presumably you will only tell her more lies.
>
> (p. 200)

The presenter is not a liar, but he has made it very difficult to understand what has happened in the session. Perhaps this confusing rendering of the session led Bion to say, "I wonder what the difficulty is?" In so doing, Bion leaves open the possibility that he is asking the presenter what *his* difficulty is (in addition to asking about the patient's difficulty).

Bion continues:

> Alternatively, is she afraid that you do *not* tell lies? If she thinks that there is a chance that you speak the truth, that would explain why she asks you what you are doing.
>
> (p. 200)

Bion is suggesting that the patient is afraid of (and, at the same time, highly values) *the way the analyst thinks* – a way of thinking that is concerned with what is true to the emotional experience that is occurring between them. What is being suggested here reflects Bion's first principle of mental functioning – the idea that the need to know the truth is the most fundamental impetus for the development of thinking. At this moment in the session, that truth involves the recognition that the patient is unable to differentiate between being awake and dreaming – that is, that the patient is psychotic.

The patient attempts to prevent the analyst from thinking, not only by surprising him by yelling at him, but also by equating thinking and "doing," and by insisting that he tell her what he is doing *immediately* – that is, without thought on his part, thereby ending genuine thinking by turning it into reflexive, fearful action. I believe that in this part of the seminar, the presenter is not only telling Bion about the very disturbing experience that he had with this patient, he is showing it to Bion (and the reader) by unwittingly making it difficult for the reader, and impossible for Bion, to differentiate between what is dream-life and what is waking life. In this way, the presenter is engendering in Bion something like the effect on him of the patient's psychosis, which the presenter is unable to think on his own.

Bion goes on:

> To put it another way: there is something wrong with this story: either the patient is lying, or she is slandering the analyst. Otherwise why should she spend her time with a dishonest liar?
>
> (p. 200)

In pointing out the contradiction that the patient views the analyst as a dishonest liar and yet continues to see him for analysis, Bion (as discussed in Chapter 5) is asking the question that he asks far more frequently than any other question in the clinical seminars: "Why has the patient come for analysis?" This question reflects the second of Bion's principles of mental functioning – the idea that it takes two minds to think one's most disturbing thoughts (and, by extension, that it is for this reason that patients come to analysis). For Bion, the omnipresent clinical question is: "What is the thought, the emotional problem, that the patient (ambivalently) is asking the analyst to help him to think?"

The seminar continues:

> Presenter: I said, "I am listening" [in response to the patient's demand to know *immediately* what the analyst was doing]. She replied, "Yes, that's important." She calmed down and continued describing her dream.
>
> Bion: That is a very interesting sequel. Notice that the analyst didn't start an argument about whether or not he is a liar [he did not angrily and fearfully offer a counterattack to the patient's attack on his thinking]; he didn't get up and leave the room [he did not evacuate thoughts in the form of action]; he didn't lose his temper [he maintained a state of mind in which he could think]. The effect

> on the patient seems to have been quite helpful. It is not a cure, but a little bit of a cure; it is enough of a cure to make another minute or two [of thinking] possible. Not only does it matter what you say or do, it also matters what you do not say or do.
>
> (pp. 200–201)

Bion, as ever, is understated in his response to the presenter. He refers to the analyst's work simply as "interesting," but nowhere else in the 52 "Clinical Seminars" does Bion step back, as he does here, to ask the other seminar members to "notice" what the analyst did in the clinical situation being discussed. Although Bion does not spell it out, I believe that what was critical to the effectiveness of the presenter's response was his calm refusal to accept the terms offered by the frightened patient (i.e. to confess or to defend himself), either of which, in this instance, would have constituted a reflexive form of non-thinking. Instead, the presenter gently, undefensively reminded the patient who he is and would continue to be – an analyst who is listening and thinking – despite the fact that the patient was frightened of the way the analyst was thinking. At the same time, she was afraid that he would not be able to remain an analyst who may be able to help her to regain her sanity by *thinking and dreaming with her* the terrifying experience that she could not think/dream on her own. In attempting to tell her dream to the analyst, the patient's capacity for thinking/dreaming fell apart – she became increasingly unable to differentiate between being awake and dreaming, and as a result she treated the analyst as if he were a figure in the dream.

How different it would have been had the presenter, instead of simply saying, "I am listening," had said, "You're afraid that I will be so frightened of you that I won't be able to think when you attack me and, as a result, I won't be able to be an analyst who will be able to help you to think your thoughts in a way that feels sane." The latter is accurate in content, but sounds to me like a rather stereotypic, analytic way of talking. In addition, I do not believe that the patient, in her state of severe distress, was capable of listening to more than the first few words of such a long and complex interpretation. By contrast, the analyst's statement, "I am listening," has the ring of words spoken by a person who is thinking and talking to another person (who is very frightened) in a manner that is genuinely his own.

The patient responded not only by saying, "Yes, that's important"; in addition, "She calmed down and continued describing her dream."

In other words, by means of the experience of having her psychotic thoughts contained by the analyst's thinking, the patient was able, if only "for another minute or two," to think (perhaps for the first time in the session).

> Presenter: She continued to describe her dream: "Mrs J wanted to come into the house and look it over. There was a portrait of a nude in one of the rooms and I knew that she would not like that. So I tried to stop her coming into the house, but I couldn't. In the kitchen there were two blood-stained garments."
>
> Bion: The patient said this was a dream. Did you believe her? It sounds very likely that she wanted to stop you from seeing what was in her mind, leaving her feeling naked. But she wasn't able to lock the door; she wasn't able to make you leave; she wasn't able to put a stop to the analysis right away. So now you may find out what kind of a person she is. However, there is always a safeguard: if you give an interpretation she can say, "It doesn't matter – I don't really think like that – it was only a dream."
>
> (p. 201)

Bion responds here by saying, "The patient said that this was a dream. Did you believe her?" Who other than Bion would have responded to "the dream" in this way? Bion's question (it seems to me) is intended to direct the presenter's attention to the fact that the patient is unable to dream, unable to distinguish between internal and external reality, and unable to distinguish between being awake and being asleep.

The patient, though seemingly describing a dream from the previous night, had not awoken from that "dream," which was not a real dream in the sense that it did not involve a differentiation of conscious and unconscious experience. It seems to me that the patient was experiencing in the session a state of mind akin to a night-terror (a phenomenon in sleep that is not a dream, but an experience of being unable to dream a terrifying experience). (See Ogden, 2004a, 2005a, for discussions of genuine dreams, night-terrors, and nightmares.) The presenter's elegant interpretation, "I am listening," had the effect of helping the patient genuinely to awaken from her dream-that-was-not-a-dream by containing the patient's unthinkable dream-thought.

Bion then addresses what he believes to be the nature of the patient's previously undreamable thought. He views the dream as an expression of the patient's belief that she is not able to distinguish her thoughts from those of the analyst and, therefore, cannot stop the analyst from "seeing what was in her mind, leaving her feeling naked." The experience of being seen naked against one's will is the opposite of feeling understood. It is closer to an experience of being raped (perhaps it is this state that is represented in the "dream" by the blood-stained garments).

Bion then makes a curious, somewhat enigmatic statement: "So now [after demonstrating to the patient that you are able to continue to think while she is yelling at you] you may find out what kind of person she is" (p. 201). I believe that Bion is suggesting that, with the help of the presenter's calm and thoughtful response to the patient's yelling at him, the non-psychotic part of the patient's personality may become a stronger force in the analysis. The non-psychotic part of the personality is that aspect of the patient that is able to think/dream, to do something uniquely her own with her lived emotional experience. In this sense, the patient, at this point in the session, may be in a position to begin to dream herself into existence, thus affording the presenter and the patient, herself, an opportunity to "find out what kind of person she is." This entire line of thought reflects Bion's fourth principle of mental functioning – the idea that even when the patient is in the grip of a full-blown psychosis, the psychoanalytic function of the personality remains operative, albeit in a highly circumscribed way. Such an assumption underlies analytic work, not only with schizophrenic and other severely disturbed patients, but also with the psychotic aspect of every patient, supervisee, or group.

But Bion cautions, "However, there is always a safeguard: if you give an interpretation she can say, 'It doesn't matter – I don't really think like that – it was only a dream.'" Here Bion is commenting on the effect of thoughts on thinking: there may be a resurgence of the patient's attack on the analyst's capacity for thinking as well as on her own. Although he does not use the term, the form of attack that Bion is describing is what he elsewhere calls *reversible perspective* (Bion, 1963, p. 50). Bion, in the clinical seminars, scrupulously avoids technical language.

The non-thinking that Bion is pointing out involves a shift of figure and ground in a way that undermines the analyst's use of his capacity for thoughtful observation: the patient claims (and believes her own claim) that when the analyst describes "the figure" (for example, an interpretation of personal meaning in a dream), the patient insists that the only reality is the ground (for example, the "nonsensical" manifest content – "it doesn't matter – I don't really think like that – it was only a dream" [p. 201]). Thus, thoughts serve to contribute not to the development of thinking, but to the destruction of thinking. From the perspective of still another of Bion's ways of conceptualizing the relationship between thoughts and thinking, the patient's thought that dreams mean nothing (the contained) is serving to destroy the capacity for patient and analyst to think together (the container). These ideas reflect Bion's third principle of mental functioning – the notion that thinking develops in order to come to terms with disturbing thoughts, and that a forceful interaction between thoughts and thinking continues throughout one's life.

The presenter continues:

> She went on, "I was afraid the house-owner wouldn't renew the contract, complaining that I didn't take care of the house – although it was in an even worse condition when I first rented it. With a magic wand she turned the nude portrait into a Negro woman dressed in a rose-coloured dress. The Negro woman started to move. I saw a door I had never seen before, opened it, and found a dying plant. I was afraid the owner would be angry because I hadn't taken care of it. I tried to revive it with the magic spell she had used, but couldn't." Then she began to shout again, "What are you doing there? You are a liar. You are doing something you don't want to tell me about. I hate you. I want to destroy you, tear you into pieces and throw the pieces away." She was very, very angry.
>
> (p. 201)

There is the same confusing ambiguity in this paragraph that there was in the opening paragraph of the seminar. Is the figure in the dream shouting at another dream figure or is the patient shouting at the analyst in waking life? (It is only the punctuation – the fact that there are double quotation marks, not single quotation marks, surrounding the words that are shouted – that indicates that it is the patient who is shouting at the presenter and not a dream figure shouting at the patient in the dream. Since Bion is listening to the presentation and not reading it, it is impossible for him to know who is shouting – the patient or a figure in the patient's dream. The distinction between being awake and being asleep is again disappearing. The patient, herself, seems to me to be disappearing. As many times as I have read the words, "I . . . found a dying plant," I still misread the words and make them say, "I . . . found a dying patient."

Bion responds to this portion of the case presentation:

> What are you doing to her? She has continued to talk, so she is taking off her own disguises. If you take off the black skin, there is a person there; if you take off the dream, she herself is there. [Perhaps Bion is suggesting that the dream is not a dream, but an assault on the non-psychotic part of the patient's personality. Without the meaning-destroying and dreamer-destroying "dream," there may be a person capable of thinking.] I think she is worried about what you are doing to her. Why do you make her speak the truth? It seems that you are only talking, but she knows it isn't only that. You are talking in some peculiar way which makes her expose the truth . . . So although it is horrible for the patient, it is just as well for the analyst to remain able to think. But we cannot settle this matter by being unable to be angry or frightened; we have to be able to have these strong feelings *and* be able to go on thinking clearly even when we have them.
>
> (p. 202)

The seminar ends with these comments by Bion. In the segment of the session that Bion is discussing, the patient becomes increasingly frightened in "the dream"/hallucination. Listening to the patient in this part of the session, for me, is like watching a person drown. The patient feels that she is dying or losing her mind – which amount to the same thing. Virtually word by word, we see the patient becoming increasingly a character in her own dream; at the same time, the figures in her dream (the landlady and the painting of the nude) are turning into living people who seem to the patient to occupy her waking life.

The published fragment of the seminar contains only a very brief account of the analytic session and does not include any of the presenter's interventions, or even his thoughts, after he said, "I am listening." This artifact of the editing and tape-recording of the seminar contributes to the distressing feeling that the patient's disintegration is not being met by further attempts on the part of the analyst to contain the patient's terror.

## Concluding comments

I will close by stating in a slightly different way what I believe to be the core principles of Bion's theory of thinking.

Thinking, for Bion, derives most fundamentally from the human need to know the truth of who one is and what is occurring in one's life. Disturbing thoughts (unprocessed experience) provide the impetus for developing an apparatus for thinking (doing psychological work with) those thoughts. There is an inborn "internal structure" for doing psychological work with our experience that Bion calls *the psychoanalytic function of the personality*. That inborn structure is analogous to the inborn "deep structure" of language (Chomsky, 1968) that underlies our capacity to learn how to speak.

In the course of a life-long process, we increasingly develop the capacity for thinking/dreaming our lived emotional experience. However, beyond a certain point (a point that varies for each individual), we find it unbearable to think/dream our experience. Under such circumstances, if we are fortunate, there is another person (perhaps a mother or father, an analyst, a supervisor, a spouse, a sibling, a close friend) who is willing and able to engage with us in a process of dreaming our formerly undreamable experience. Dreaming – whether on our own or with another person – is our most profound form of thinking: it is the principal medium in which we do the psychological work of being and becoming human in the process of attempting to face the reality of, and come to terms with, our emotional problems.

# 7

# Reading Loewald: Oedipus reconceived

Freud's Oedipus complex has, in the history of psychoanalysis, been reinvented several times – for example, by Klein, Fairbairn, Lacan, and Kohut. At the heart of Loewald's (1979) re-conceptualization of the Oedipus complex is the idea that it is the task of each new generation to make use of, destroy, and reinvent the creations of the previous generation. Loewald reformulates the Oedipus complex in a way that provides fresh ways of viewing many of the fundamental human tasks entailed in growing up, growing old, and, in between the two, managing to make something of one's own that succeeding generations might make use of to create something unique of their own. Thus, Loewald reinvents Freud's version of the Oedipus complex, and it is my task to re-conceive Loewald's version of the Oedipus complex in the very act of presenting it. By means of a close reading of Loewald's (1979) "The Waning of the Oedipus Complex," I will demonstrate what it is about the way Loewald thinks that leads me to view that paper as a watershed in the development of psychoanalytic thought.

The sequential nature of narrative writing makes it difficult for Loewald to capture the simultaneity of the elements of the Oedipus complex; I, too, must struggle with this dilemma. I have elected to discuss Loewald's overlapping ideas in more or less the sequence he presents them, addressing the tension between influence and originality in the succession of generations; the murder of the oedipal parents and the appropriation of their authority; the metamorphic internalization of the child's experience of the parents, which underlies the formation of a self responsible for itself and to itself; and the transitional incestuous object relationship that mediates the dialectical interplay between differentiated and undifferentiated forms of object relatedness. I will conclude with a comparison of Freud's and Loewald's conceptions of the Oedipus complex.

## Freud's theory of the Oedipus complex

In order to place Loewald's contribution in context, I will review the major tenets of Freud's Oedipus complex, as I understand them. Freud's conception of the Oedipus complex is built on a foundation of four revolutionary ideas: (1) All of human psychology and psychopathology, as well as all human cultural achievements, can be understood in terms of urges and meanings that have their roots in the sexual and aggressive instincts. (2) The sexual instinct is experienced as a driving force beginning at birth and is elaborated sequentially in its oral, anal, and phallic components in the course of the first five years of life. (3) Of the multitude of myths and stories that human beings have created, the myth of Oedipus, for psychoanalysis, is the single most important narrative organizing human psychological development. (4) The triangulated set of conflictual murderous and incestuous fantasies constituting the Oedipus complex is "determined and laid down by heredity" (Freud, 1924, p. 174) – that is, it is a manifestation of a universal, inborn propensity of human beings to organize experience in this particular way (see Ogden, 1986a).

The Oedipus complex for Freud (1924) is "contemporaneous" (p. 174) with the phallic phase of sexual development. It is a web of intrapsychic and interpersonal parent–child relationships in which the boy, for example, takes his mother as the object of his romantic and sexual desire, and wishes to take his father's place with his mother (Freud, 1910, 1921, 1923, 1924, 1925). The father is simultaneously admired and viewed as a punitive rival. The aggressive instinct is manifested, for the boy, in the form of the wish to kill his father in order to have his mother for himself. The wish to kill the father is a highly ambivalent one, given the boy's pre-oedipal love for and identification with his father, as well as the boy's erotic attachment to his father in the negative Oedipus complex (Freud, 1921). The boy experiences guilt in response to his wish to murder his father (in the positive Oedipus complex) and his mother (in the negative Oedipus complex). Similarly, the girl takes her father as the object of her desire and wishes to take her mother's place with her father. She, too, experiences guilt in response to her incestuous and murderous wishes in the complete Oedipus complex (Freud, 1921, 1925).

The child guiltily fears punishment for his or her murderous and incestuous wishes in the form of castration at the hands of the father. Whether or not actual castration threats are made, the threat of castration is present in the mind of the child as a "primal phantasy" (Freud, 1916–1917, p. 370), a universal unconscious fantasy that is part of the make-up of the human psyche.

"Analytic observation[s] . . . justify the statement that the destruction of the Oedipus complex is brought about by the threat of castration" (Freud, 1924, p. 177). That is, the child, for fear of punishment in the form of castration, relinquishes his or her sexual and aggressive strivings in relation to the oedipal parents and replaces those "object cathexes . . . [with] identifications" (Freud, 1924, p. 176) with parental authority, prohibitions, and ideals, which form the core of a new psychic structure, the superego.

## The tension between influence and originality

With Freud's conception of the Oedipus complex in mind, I will now turn to Loewald's reformulation. The opening sentence of Loewald's paper is a curious one in that it appears to make no reference to the subject that the paper will address: "Many of the views expressed in this paper have been stated previously by others" (Loewald, 1979, p. 384).[1] Why would anyone begin a psychoanalytic paper with a disclaimer renouncing claims for originality? Loewald goes on immediately (still not giving the reader a rationale for his odd approach) to cite a lengthy passage from Breuer's introduction to the theoretical section of *Studies on Hysteria*:

> When a science is making rapid advances, thoughts which were first expressed by single individuals quickly become common property. Thus no one who attempts to put forward today his views on hysteria and its psychical basis can avoid repeating a great quantity of other people's thoughts, which are in the act of passing from personal into general possession. It is scarcely possible always

[1] All page references in this chapter not otherwise specified refer to Loewald's (1979) "The Waning of the Oedipus Complex."

> to be certain who first gave them utterance, and there is always a danger of regarding as a product of one's own what has already been said by someone else. I hope, therefore, that I may be excused if few quotations are found in this discussion and if no strict distinction is made between what is my own and what originates elsewhere. Originality is claimed for very little of what will be found in the following pages.
>
> (Breuer and Freud, 1893–1895, pp. 185–186; cited by Loewald, 1979, p. 384)

Subliminally, a sense of cyclical time is created by the juxtaposition of Loewald's disclaiming originality and Breuer's virtually identical statement made almost a century earlier. Loewald, before discussing his ideas concerning the Oedipus complex, is *showing* them to us in our experience of reading: no generation has the right to claim absolute originality for its creations (see Ogden, 2003b, 2005b). And yet, each new generation does contribute something uniquely of its own: "Many [*not all*] of the views expressed in this paper have been stated previously" (Loewald); and "Originality is claimed for very little [*but something*]" (Breuer).[2]

Between the lines of Loewald's text is the idea that it is the fate of the child (as it was the fate of the parents) that what he makes of his own will enter a process of "passing from personal into general possession" (Breuer). In other words, what we do manage to create that bears our own mark will become part of the pool of collective knowledge, and, in so doing, we become nameless, but not insignificant ancestors to succeeding generations: "there is always a danger of regarding as a product of one's own what has already been said by someone else" (Breuer), an ancestor whose name has been lost to us.

Loewald's paper goes on to explore and bring to life this tension between one's indebtedness to one's forbears and one's wish to free oneself from them in the process of becoming a person in one's own terms. This tension between influence and originality lies at the core of the Oedipus complex, as Loewald conceives of it.

[2] Breuer's words echo those written by Plato two-and-a-half millennia earlier: "Now I am well aware that none of these ideas can have come from me – I know my own ignorance. The only other possibility, I think, is that I was filled, like an empty jar, by the words of other people streaming in through my ears, though I'm so stupid that I've even forgotten where and from whom I heard them" (Plato, 1997, p. 514). Loewald, trained in philosophy, no doubt was familiar with this dialogue.

## More than a repression

Loewald's paper seems to begin again in its second paragraph with a definition of the Oedipus complex as the "psychic representation of a central, instinctually motivated, triangular conflictual constellation of child–parent relations" (p. 384). (With its several beginnings and several endings, the paper itself embodies the multiplicity of births and deaths that mark the endless cycle of generations.) Loewald then draws our attention to the way in which Freud (1923, 1925), in speaking of the fate of the Oedipus complex, uses forceful language, referring to its "destruction" (1924, p. 177) and its "demolition" (Freud, 1925, p. 257). Moreover, Freud (1924) insists, "If the ego has . . . not achieved much more than a *repression* of the complex, the latter persists in an unconscious state . . . and will later manifest its pathogenic effect" (p. 177). This idea provides Loewald the key to his understanding of the fate of the Oedipus complex.

The reader's head begins to swim at this point as a consequence of the convergence of two interrelated enigmatic ideas: (1) the notion that the Oedipus complex is "demolished" (how are we to understand the idea that some of the most important human experiences are, in health, destroyed?); and (2) the idea that the demolition of the Oedipus complex is "more than a repression" (whatever that means). The reader, here and throughout the paper, must do a good deal of thinking for himself in making something of his own with the ideas that Loewald is presenting. This, after all, is the task of each new generation vis-à-vis the creations of its ancestors.

In an effort to find his bearings in this portion of the paper, the reader must grapple with several questions. To begin with, the reader must determine the meaning of the term *repression* as it is being used here. Freud uses the term to refer to two overlapping but distinct ideas in the course of his writing. At times, he uses the term to refer to psychological operations that serve to establish "the unconscious as a domain separate from the rest of the psyche" (Laplanche and Pontalis, 1967, p. 390), a sine qua non of psychological health. At other times – including, I believe, the instance under discussion – the term is used to refer to a pathogenic expulsion from consciousness of disturbing thoughts and feelings. Not only is the repressed segregated from the main body of conscious thought, repressed thoughts and feelings are for the most part cut off from conscious and unconscious psychological work.

The reader must also attempt to formulate for himself what it means to bring the Oedipus complex to a close, not by repressing it, but by demolishing the thoughts, feelings, bodily sensations, and object-related experiences that constitute it. To my mind – and I think that there would be general agreement among psychoanalysts on this point – the psychic registration of a significant experience, whether that registration be conscious or unconscious, is never destroyed. It may be suppressed, repressed, displaced, denied, disowned, dissociated, projected, introjected, split off, foreclosed, and so on, but never destroyed or demolished. No experience can ever "unhappen" psychically. And yet this is what Freud and Loewald are insisting to be the case – at least to a significant degree – in the waning of the Oedipus complex. The unresolved question of what it means to say that the Oedipus complex undergoes "more than a repression" (i.e. that it is demolished) generates in the experience of reading Loewald's paper a tension that is not unlike the experience of living with unresolved (but not repressed) oedipal conflict. It unsettles everything it touches in a vitalizing way.

## Parricide: a loving murder

Having introduced these thoughts and questions regarding the demolition of the Oedipus complex, Loewald proceeds to broaden the traditional conception of the oedipal murder. He uses the term *parricide* to refer to the act committed by "One who murders a person to whom he stands in a specially sacred relation, as a father, mother, or other near relative, or (in a wider sense) a ruler. Sometimes, one guilty of treason (*Webster, International Dictionary, 2nd ed.*)" (cited by Loewald, 1979, p. 387).[3] In the act of parricide, Loewald observes,

> It is a parental authority that is murdered; by that, whatever is sacred about the bond between child and parent is violated. If we take etymology as a guide, it is bringing forth, nourishing, providing for, and protecting of the child by the parents that constitute their

[3] Loewald uses the word *sacred* as a secular term to refer to that which is solemnly, respectfully set apart, as poetry, for Plato and Borges, is set apart from other forms of human expressiveness – poetry is "something winged, light and sacred" (Plato, cited by Borges, 1984, p. 32).

> parenthood, authority (authorship), and render sacred the child's ties with the parents. Parricide is a crime against the sanctity of such a bond.
>
> (p. 387)

Loewald again and again in his paper makes use of etymology – the ancestry of words, the history of the way succeeding generations both draw upon and alter the meanings of words.

Parricide involves a revolt against parental authority and parental claims to authorship of the child. That revolt involves not a ceremonious passing of the baton from one generation to the next, but a murder in which a sacred bond is severed. The child's breaking of the sacred bond to the parents does not represent a fearful response to the threat of bodily mutilation (castration), but a passionate assertion of the "active urge for emancipation" (p. 389) from the parents. Loewald's phrase *urge for emancipation* connects the word *urge* (which has a strong tie to the bodily instinctual drives) with the word *emancipation*, thus generating the idea of an innate drive for individuation. In the language itself, instinct theory is being broadened by Loewald to include drives beyond the sexual and aggressive urges (see Chodorow, 2003; Kaywin, 1993; and Mitchell, 1998, for discussions of the relationship between instinct theory and object relations theory in Loewald's work).

In the oedipal battle, "opponents are required" (p. 389). A relative absence of genuine parental authority leaves the child with little to appropriate. Moreover, when the parents' authority has not been established, the child's fantasies lack "brakes" (Winnicott, 1945, p. 153) – that is, the secure knowledge that his fantasies will not be allowed to be played out in reality. When parental authority does not provide the "brakes" for fantasy, the fantasied murder of those one loves and depends upon is too frightening to endure. Under such pathological circumstances, the child, in an effort to defend himself against the danger of the actual murder of the parents, represses (buries alive) his murderous impulses and enforces that repression by adopting a harshly punitive stance toward these feelings. In health, paradoxically, the felt presence of parental authority makes it possible for the child to safely murder his parents psychically (a fantasy that need not be repressed). Oedipal parricide does not require repression because it is ultimately a loving act, a "passionate appropriation of what is experienced as loveable and admirable in parents" (p. 396). In a sense, the fantasied death of one's oedipal parents is "collateral damage" in the child's struggle for independence and individuation. Killing one's parents is not an end in itself.

For Loewald, the Oedipus complex is at its core a face-off between the generations, a life-and-death battle for autonomy, authority, and responsibility. In this struggle, parents are "actively rejected, fought against, and destroyed, to varying degrees" (pp. 388–389). Difficulty arises not from parricidal fantasies per se, but from an inability to safely commit parricide, to sever one's oedipal ties to one's parents. The following brief clinical account illustrates a form of difficulty encountered in the oedipal appropriation of parental authority.

Several years into his analysis, Mr N told me the following dream:

> "I was checking in at the front desk of a hotel late at night. The man behind the desk told me that all the rooms were booked. I said that I had heard that hotels keep a few rooms open in case someone shows up in the middle of the night. I thought, but did not say to him, that those rooms are meant for important people. I knew that I was not an important person. At the other end of the long desk, an older woman who was checking in, said in a commanding voice, 'He's with me – he'll share my room.' I didn't want to share a room with her. The thought was repellent. I felt as if I couldn't get a breath of air and tried to find a way out of the hotel, but I couldn't find an exit."
>
> Mr N said that he felt extremely embarrassed by the dream and had considered not mentioning it to me. He told me that even though we had often talked about his feeling that his parents had had no psychological room in themselves for him as a child, he was horrified in the dream by the woman (who seemed like his mother) offering to have him share her room and, by implication, her bed with him.
>
> I said to Mr N that the embarrassment he felt in response to the dream may stem not only from his feeling horrified by the idea of sleeping with his mother, but also from seeing himself as a perennial child who lacks the authority to claim a place of his own among adults – a boy who will never become a man.

By contrast, an experience in the analysis of a man in his mid-20s captures something of the experience of a healthy oedipal succession of generations:

> A medical student near the end of his analysis with me began affectionately to refer to me as "a geezer" after it had become apparent that I knew very little of the developments in psychopharmacology that had occurred in the previous twenty-five years. I was reminded of my own first analysis, which had begun while I was a medical student. My analyst occasionally referred to himself as an "old buck" in response to my competitiveness with him regarding what I was learning about current developments in psychoanalysis. I remembered having been surprised by his seemingly calm acceptance of his place in the "over-the-hill" generation of analysts and of my place in the new (and, I believed, far more dynamic) generation.
>
> While with my medical student analysand, my memory of my analyst's referring to himself as an old buck struck me as both comic and disturbing – disturbing in that, at the time he said it, he was younger than I was at that juncture in the analysis of my patient. I recognized how his acceptance of his place in the succession of generations was currently of great value to me in my efforts not only to accept, but also, in a certain way, to embrace my place as "a geezer" in the analysis of my medical student.

As parents to our children, even as we fight to maintain our parental authority, we allow ourselves to be killed by our children lest we "diminish them" (p. 395). In the Oedipus myth, Laius and Jocasta are told by the oracle at Delphi that their son is destined to murder his father. The horror of this prophecy is equivalent in present-day terms to a hospital forewarning each couple as they enter the obstetrics ward that their child who is about to be born will one day murder them. Laius and Jocasta attempt to circumvent such an outcome by killing their child. But they cannot bring themselves to commit the murder by their own hand. They give Oedipus to a shepherd who is told to leave the infant in the forest to die. In so doing, Laius and Jocasta unconsciously collude in their own murder. They create a window of opportunity for their child not only to survive, but also to grow up to murder them.[4]

The dilemma faced by Laius and Jocasta is a dilemma shared not only by all parents, but also by all analysts when we begin analysis with a new patient. In beginning analysis, we as analysts are setting in

[4] The Oedipus complex is, in a sense, a process by which the child, in killing his parents (with their cooperation), creates his own ancestors (see Borges, 1962).

motion a process in which the patient – if all goes well – will contribute to our dying. For all to go well, we must allow ourselves to be killed by our patients lest "we diminish them" (p. 395), for example, by treating them as less mature than they are, by giving advice that is not needed, supportive tones of voice that are unwanted, and interpretations that are undermining of the patient's ability to think reflectively and insightfully for himself. Not to diminish one's children (and one's patients) involves not a passive resignation to aging and death, but an actively loving gesture repeated time and again in which one gives over one's place in the present generation to take one's place sadly and proudly among those in the process of becoming ancestors. Resistance to taking one's place as part of the past generation will not stop the succession of generations, but it will leave a felt absence in the lives of one's children and grandchildren, an absence where their ancestors might under other circumstances have been a highly valued presence. (Loewald told his colleague Bryce Boyer that he could not have written this paper before he became a grandfather [Boyer, 1999, personal communication].)

Parents may try to protect themselves against giving way to the next generation by behaving as if there is no difference between the generations. For example, when parents do not close bedroom and bathroom doors, or display erotic photographs as "art," or do not wear clothing at home because "the human body is not a shameful thing," they are implicitly claiming that there is no generational difference – children and adults are equal. Children, under such circumstances, have no genuine parental objects to kill and only a perverse version of parental authority to appropriate. This leaves the individual a stunted child frozen in time.

Having discussed the central role in the Oedipus complex of the child's loving murder of his parents, Loewald makes a remarkable statement that sets this paper apart from its psychoanalytic predecessors:

> If we do not shrink from blunt language, in our role as children of our parents, by genuine emancipation we do kill something vital in them – not all in one blow and not in all respects, but contributing to their dying.
>
> (p. 395)

In the space of a single sentence, the Oedipus complex is radically reconceived. It had been well established by Freud (1909, 1910) that the Oedipus complex is not simply an intrapsychic event, but a set of living object relationships between the child and his parents. But Loewald does not stop there. For him, the fantasied murder of the parents that is played out in oedipal object relationships contributes to – is part of the process of – the parents' dying. It is tempting to water down Loewald's "blunt language" by saying that "their dying" is a metaphor for parents' relinquishing their authority over (their authorship of) the life of the child. But Loewald is saying more than that: he is insisting that the living out of the Oedipus complex by children and their parents is part of the emotional process (which is inseparable from bodily processes) by which human beings grow up, grow old, and die.

The battle between parents and children for autonomy and authority is most evident in adolescence and beyond, but it is, of course, equally important in early childhood. This is true not only of the child's falling in love with one parent while becoming intensely jealous of, and rivalrous with, the other. In addition, for example, the "terrible twos" often involves the parents in a battle with their newly ambulatory child who is relentlessly insistent on his independence. Parents of two-year-olds frequently experience their child's "stubborn willfulness" as a betrayal of an unspoken agreement that the child will remain a fully dependent, adored, and adoring baby "forever." The child's breaking of the "agreement" constitutes an assault on the parents' wish to remain parents of a baby timelessly – that is, insulated from the passage of time, aging, death, and the succession of generations. (The relationship of the "stubborn" toddler to his parents is triangulated to the degree that the child splits the parents intrapsychically into the good and the bad parent or parents.)

## The metamorphic internalization of the oedipal parents

Thus, parricide, from the point of view both of parents and of children, is a necessary path to the child's growing up, his coming to life as an adult who has attained authority in his own right. Oedipal parricide conceived of in this way underlies, for both Freud and Loewald, the organization of "the superego [which is] the culmination of individual psychic structure formation" (Loewald, 1979, p. 404). The use of the term *superego* in this phrase and throughout Loewald's paper represents a residue of the structural model of the mind that Loewald is in the process of transforming. Consequently, the term, as used by Loewald, is confusing. As I read his paper, I find it clarifying to my thinking to "translate" the term *superego* into terms that are more in keeping with the ideas that Loewald is developing. In place of the word *superego*, I use the idea of an aspect of the self (derived from appropriated parental authority) that takes the measure of, and the responsibility for, who one is and how one conducts oneself.

Superego formation involves an "internalization" (Loewald, 1979, p. 390) of or "identification" (p. 391) with the oedipal parents. Freud [1921, 1923, 1924, 1925], too, repeatedly uses the terms *identification*, *introjection*, and *incorporation* to describe the process of superego formation. This process brings us to what I consider to be one of the most difficult and most important questions raised by Loewald regarding the Oedipus complex: What does it mean to say that oedipal object relationships are internalized in the process of superego organization? Loewald responds to this question in a very dense passage that leaves a great deal unsaid or merely suggested. I will offer a close reading of this passage in which I include inferences that I have drawn from Loewald's statements:

> The organization of the superego, as internalization . . . of oedipal object relations, documents parricide and at the same time is its atonement and metamorphosis: atonement insofar as the superego makes up for and is a restitution of oedipal relationships; metamorphosis insofar as in this restitution oedipal object relations are transmuted into internal, intrapsychic structural relations.
>
> (p. 389)

To paraphrase the opening portion of this passage, the organization of the superego "documents" parricide in the sense that superego organization is living proof of the murder of the parents. The superego embodies the child's successful appropriation of parental authority, which is transformed into the child's capacities for autonomy and responsibility. The superego as psychic structure monitors the ego and, in this sense, takes responsibility for the ego/"*das Ich*" "the I".

That same process of superego organization not only constitutes an internal record of parricide in the form of an alteration of the psyche of the child, it also constitutes an "atonement" (p. 389) for the murder of the parents. As I understand it, the organization of the superego represents an atonement for parricide in that, at the same moment that the child murders the parents (psychically), he bestows upon them a form of immortality. That is, by incorporating the child's experience of his parents (albeit a "transmuted" version of them) into the very structure of who he is as an individual, the child secures the parents a place, a seat of influence, not only in the way the child conducts his life, but also in the way the child's children conduct their lives, and on and on. I am using the word *children*, here, both literally and metaphorically. The alteration of the psyche involved in superego organization influences not simply the way the grown child relates to his own children, it affects everything that the child creates in the course of his life – for example, the qualities of the friendships and other love relationships in which he takes part, as well as the thinking and creativity that he brings to the work that he does. These creations (his literal and metaphorical children) alter those they touch, who, in turn, alter those they touch.

The "internalization" of the parents (in a transformed state) constitutes atonement for killing the parents in that this internalization contributes to the child's becoming like the parents. But, in another sense, it is in the "transmutation" of the parents that an even more profound form of atonement lies. To the extent that the parents have been transformed in the internalization process, the parents have contributed to the creation of a child who is capable of being and becoming *unlike them* – that is, capable of becoming a person who is, in certain respects, more than the people who the parents have been capable of being and becoming. What more meaningful atonement can there be for killing one's parents?

Loewald continues in the passage under discussion: superego organization is an atonement for parricide "insofar as the superego makes up for and is a restitution of oedipal object relations." These words are carefully chosen. The word *restitution* derives from the Latin word meaning *to re-establish*. The formation of the superego restores to the parents their authority as parents – but not the same authority that they formerly held as parents. Now they are parents to a child who is increasingly capable of being responsible for himself and to himself as an autonomous person. The parents who are "restituted" (re-established) are parents who had not previously existed (or, perhaps more accurately, had existed only as a potential).

For Loewald, in the passage under discussion, superego formation as a part of the resolution of the Oedipus complex represents not only an atonement for parricide and the restitution of the parents, but also a "metamorphosis insofar as in this restitution oedipal object relations are transmuted into internal, intrapsychic structural relations" (p. 389). I find the metaphor of metamorphosis to be critical to Loewald's conception of what it means to say that the parents are internalized in a "transmuted" form. (Loewald, in this paper, uses the word *metamorphosis* only in the sentence being cited and may not have been aware of the full implications of his use of this metaphor.) In complete metamorphosis (for example, in the life cycle of the butterfly), inside the cocoon, the tissues of the caterpillar (the larva) break down. A few clusters of cells from the breakdown of the larval tissues constitute the beginning of a new cellular organization from which adult structures are generated (e.g. wings, eyes, tongue, antennae, and body segments).

There is continuity (the DNA of the caterpillar and that of the butterfly are identical) and discontinuity (there is a vast difference between the morphology and physiology of the external and internal structures of the caterpillar and those of the butterfly). So, too, superego formation (the internalization of oedipal object relations) involves a simultaneity of continuity and radical transformation. The parents (as experienced by the child) are not internalized, any more than a caterpillar sprouts wings. The child's "internalization" of oedipal object relationships involves a profound transformation of his experience of his parents (analogous to the breakdown of the bodily structure of the caterpillar) before they are restituted in the form of the organization of the child's more mature psychic structure (superego formation).[5]

In other words, the child's "internalized" Oedipal object relationships (constituting the superego) have their origins in the "DNA" of the parents – that is, the unconscious psychological make-up of the

[5] A passage from Karp and Berrill's (1981) classic, *Development*, underscores the aptness of the metaphor of metamorphosis:

> The completion of the cocoon signals the beginning of a new and even more remarkable sequence of events. On the third day after a cocoon is finished, a great wave of death and destruction sweeps over the internal organs of the caterpillar. The specialized larval tissues break down, but meanwhile, certain more or less discrete clusters of cells, tucked away here and there in the body, begin to grow rapidly, nourishing themselves on the breakdown products of the dead and dying larval tissues. These are the imaginal discs. . . . Their spurt of growth now shapes the organism according to a new plan. New organs arise from the discs.
>
> (p. 692)

parents (which in turn "documents" their own oedipal object relationships with their parents). At the same time, despite this powerful transgenerational continuity of oedipal experience, if the child (with the parents' help) is able to kill his oedipal parents, he creates a psychological clearance in which to enter into libidinal relationships with "novel" (p. 390) (non-incestuous) objects. These novel relationships have a life of their own outside of the terms of the child's libidinal and aggressive relationships with his oedipal parents. In this way, genuinely novel (non-incestuous) relationships with one's parents and others become possible. (The novel object relationships are colored by, but not dominated by, transferences to the oedipal parents.)

In a single summary sentence, which could have been written by no one other than Loewald, the elements of the transformations involved in superego formation (the establishment of an autonomous, responsible self) are brought together: "The self, in its autonomy, is an atonement structure, a structure of reconciliation, and as such a supreme achievement" (p. 394).

## The transitional incestuous object relationship

The paper begins anew as Loewald takes up the incestuous component of the Oedipus complex. This portion of the paper, for me, lacks the power of the foregoing discussion of imagined (and real) parricide, guilt, atonement, and restitution. It seems to me that the centerpiece of the paper – and Loewald's principal interest – is the role of the Oedipus complex in the child's achievement of an autonomous, responsible self. Incestuous desire is a subsidiary theme in that story.

Loewald opens his discussion of oedipal incestuous wishes by raising the rarely asked (even a bit startling) question: "What's wrong with incest?" He responds, "Incestuous object relations are evil, according to received morality, in that they interfere with or destroy that sacred bond . . . the original oneness, most obvious in the mother–infant dual unity" (p. 396). Incest involves the intrusion of differentiated libidinal object relatedness into the " 'sacred' innocence of primary narcissistic unity . . . [which is] anterior to individuation and its inherent guilt and atonement" (p. 396).

In other words, we view incest as evil because, in incest, differentiated, object-related sexual desire is directed toward the very same person (and the very same body) with whom an undifferentiated bond (which we hold sacred) existed and continues to exist. Thus, for Loewald, incest is felt to be wrong, not primarily because it represents a challenge to the father's authority and claim to the mother, or because it denies the difference between the generations, but because it destroys the demarcation between a fused form of mother–child relatedness (primary identification) and a differentiated object relatedness with the same person. Incest is felt to be evil because it overturns the "barrier between [primary] identification [at-one-ment] and [differentiated] object cathexis" (p. 397).

The overturning of the barrier between primary identification and object cathexis is a matter of the greatest importance, not only because the individual's emerging sexuality is shaped by the way the parents and children handle incestuous desire, but, perhaps even more importantly, because the individual's capacity for healthy object relatedness of every sort – his capacity to establish a generative dialectic of separateness from, and union with, other people – depends upon the living integrity of that barrier.

Parricide is a manifestation of the oedipal child's drive to become an autonomous individual; incestuous wishes and fantasies represent the concurrent need on the part of the oedipal child for unity with the mother. From this vantage point, "The incestuous [oedipal] object thus is an intermediate, ambiguous entity, neither a full-fledged libidinal *objectum* [differentiated object] nor an unequivocal *identificatum* [undifferentiated object]" (p. 397). Loewald uses the terms *incestuous object* and *incestuous object relationship* to refer not to actual incest, but to external and internal object relationships in which incestuous fantasies predominate. The incestuous oedipal relationship persists as an ongoing aspect of the Oedipus complex, which mediates the tension between the urge for autonomy and responsibility and the healthy pull toward unity (for example, as an aspect of falling in love, empathy, sexuality, care giving, "primary maternal preoccupation" [Winnicott, 1956, p. 300], and so on).

Both the superego and the transitional incestuous object relationship are heirs to the Oedipus complex in complementary ways, each mediating a tension between love of the parents and the wish to emancipate oneself from them and to establish novel object relationships. There are, however, important differences between the two. The atonement (at-one-ment) that underlies superego formation involves the metamorphic internalization of an object relationship with the parents as whole and separate objects; by contrast, the at-one-ment involved in (transitional) incestuous object relatedness is that of fusion with the parents (primary identification).

By understanding the oedipal incestuous object relationship as constituting an intermediate position between undifferentiated and differentiated object relatedness, Loewald is not simply amplifying a psychoanalytic conception of pre-oedipal development. He is suggesting something more. The Oedipus complex is not only a set of differentiated object relationships that comprise "the neurotic core" (p. 400) of the personality. The Oedipus complex "contains . . . in its very core" (p. 399) a more archaic set of object relationships that constitutes the "psychotic core" (p. 400) of the personality. From the latter, the earliest forms of healthy separation–individuation emerge.

Thus, the Oedipus complex is the emotional crucible in which the entirety of the personality is forged as the oedipal configuration is reworked and reorganized on increasingly more mature planes throughout the individual's life (see Ogden, 1987). Loewald, not one to claim originality for his ideas, states that while Freud "acknowledged the fact [that the Oedipus complex centrally involves undifferentiated object relations] long ago" (Loewald, 1979, p. 399), this aspect of the Oedipus complex is "more [important] than was realized by Freud" (p. 399). This more primitive aspect of the Oedipus complex is not outgrown; rather, it takes its place as "a deep layer of advanced mentality" (p. 402).

Before concluding this part of the discussion, I will revisit an idea that remains unresolved. At the outset of the paper, Loewald (with Freud) insisted that in health the Oedipus complex is "demolished." Loewald, in the course of the paper, modifies that idea:

> In the abstract, as the organization of this structure [the autonomous self] proceeds, the Oedipus complex would be destroyed as a constellation of object relations or their fantasy representations. But, in the words of Ariel in Shakespeare's *Tempest*, nothing fades, "but doth suffer a sea-change into something rich and strange."
> (p. 394)

In other words, the Oedipus complex is not destroyed, but is continually in the process of being transformed into "something rich and strange" – that is, into a multitude of evolving, forever-problematic aspects of the human condition that constitute "the troubling but rewarding richness of life" (p. 400). The reader may wonder why

Loewald does not say so from the beginning instead of invoking the clearly untenable idea that experience can be destroyed. I believe that Loewald begins with the more absolute and dramatic language because there is a truth to it that he does not want the reader to lose sight of: to the degree that one succeeds in murdering one's parents psychically and atones for that parricide in a way that contributes to the formation of an autonomous self, one is released from the emotional confines of the Oedipus complex. The Oedipus complex is destroyed to the extent that oedipal relationships with one's parents no longer constitute the conscious and unconscious emotional world within which the individual lives as a perennial, dependent child.

The paper closes as it began, with a comment addressing writing itself as opposed to the subject matter that has been taken up:

> I am aware that, perhaps confusingly, I have shifted perspectives several times in my presentation. I hope that the composite picture I have tried to sketch in this fashion has not become too blurred by my approach.
>
> (p. 404)

The words *shift[ing] perspectives*, to my ear, describe a style of writing and thinking that is always in the process of being revised, and a style of reading that is as critically questioning as it is receptive to the ideas being presented. What more suitable ending can one imagine for a paper that addresses the ways in which one generation leaves its mark on the next, and yet fosters in its descendants the exercise of their right and responsibility to become authors of their own ideas and ways of conducting themselves?

## Loewald and Freud

I will conclude by highlighting some of the differences between Loewald's and Freud's conceptions of the Oedipus complex. For Loewald, the Oedipus complex is driven not primarily by the child's sexual and aggressive impulses (as it is for Freud), but by the "urge for emancipation," the need to become an autonomous individual. The girl, for example, is not most fundamentally driven to take the place of her mother in the parents' bed, but to take her parents' authority as her own. The child atones for imagined (and real) parricide by means of a metamorphic internalization of the oedipal parents, which results in an alteration of the self (the formation of a new psychic agency, the superego). "Responsibility to oneself . . . is the essence of superego as internal agency" (Loewald, 1979, p. 392). Thus, the child repays the parents in the most meaningful terms possible – that is, by establishing a sense of self that is responsible to oneself and for oneself, a self that may be capable of becoming a person who is, in ways, more than the people who the parents were capable of being and becoming.

The incestuous component of the Oedipus complex contributes to the maturation of the self by serving as an ambiguous, transitional form of object relatedness that holds in tension with one another differentiated and undifferentiated dimensions of mature object ties. The Oedipus complex is brought to an end not by a fear-driven response to the threat of castration, but by the child's need to atone for parricide and to restore to the parents their (now transformed) authority as parents.

I do not view Loewald's version of the Oedipus complex as an updated version of Freud's. Rather, to my mind, the two renderings of the Oedipus complex constitute different perspectives from which to view the same phenomena. Both perspectives are indispensable to a contemporary psychoanalytic understanding of the Oedipus complex.

# 8

# Reading Harold Searles

Harold Searles, to my mind, is unrivaled in his ability to capture in words his observations concerning his emotional response to what is occurring in the analytic relationship and his use of these observations in his effort to understand and interpret the transference-countertransference. I will offer close readings of portions of two of Searles's papers, "Oedipal Love in the Countertransference" (1959) and "Unconscious Identification" (1990), in which I describe not only *what* Searles thinks, but what I believe to be the essence of *the way* Searles thinks and *how* he works in the analytic setting. Being receptive to what is occurring at a given moment in an analysis involves, for Searles, an exquisite sensitivity to the unconscious communications of the patient. Such receptivity to the patient's unconscious communications requires of the analyst a form of laying bare his own unconscious experience. Searles's way of using himself analytically very often entails a blurring of the distinction between his own conscious and unconscious experience as well as the distinction between his unconscious experience and that of the patient. As a result, Searles's comments to the patient (and to the reader) concerning what he understands to be occurring between himself and the patient are often startling to the reader, but almost always utilizable by the patient (and the reader) for purposes of conscious and unconscious psychological work.

In discussing "Oedipal Love in the Countertransference," I will focus on the way in which, for Searles, unflinchingly accurate clinical observation spawns original clinical theory (in this instance, a reconceptualization of the Oedipus complex). When I speak of *clinical theory*, I am referring to proposed experience-near understandings (formulated in terms of thoughts, feelings, and behavior) of phenomena occurring in the clinical setting. Transference, for example, is a clinical theory that proposes that certain of the patient's feelings towards the analyst, unbeknownst to the patient, have their origins in feelings that the patient experienced in previous real and imagined object relationships, usually childhood relationships. By contrast, psychoanalytic theories involving higher levels of abstraction (for example, Freud's topographic model, Klein's concept of the internal object world, and Bion's theory of alpha function) propose spatial and other types of metaphor as ways of thinking about how the mind works.

In my reading of "Unconscious Identification," I suggest that Searles has a distinctive way of thinking and working analytically that might be thought of as a process of "turning experience inside out." By this I mean that Searles transforms what had been an invisible, and yet felt, presence, an emotional context, into psychological content about which the patient may be able to think and speak. What had been a frightening, unnamed, fully taken-for-granted quality of the patient's internal and external world is transformed by Searles into a verbally symbolized emotional dilemma about which the analytic pair may be able to think and converse.

Finally, I will discuss what I view as the complementarity between Searles's work and that of Bion. I have found that reading Searles provides a vibrant clinical context for Bion's work, and reading Bion provides a valuable theoretical context for Searles's work. I will focus, in particular, on the mutually enriching "conversation" (created in the mind of the reader) between Searles's clinical work and Bion's concepts of the container-contained, the fundamental human need for truth, and Bion's reconceptualization of the relationship between conscious and unconscious experience.

## Oedipal love in the countertransference

In the opening pages of the "Oedipal Love" paper, Searles provides a thoughtful review of the analytic literature concerning countertransference love. The consensus on this topic current at the time was succinctly articulated by Tower (1956, cited by Searles, 1959, p. 285): "Virtually every writer on the subject of countertransference . . . states unequivocally that no form of erotic reaction to a patient is to be tolerated. . . ." With this sentiment looming in the background,

Searles presents an analytic experience that occurred in the latter part of a four-year analysis (which he conducted early in his career). He tells us that the patient's femininity had initially been "considerably repressed" (1959, p. 290). In the last year of this analysis, Searles found himself "having . . . abundant desires to be married to her, and fantasies of being her husband" (p. 290). Blunt acknowledgment of such thoughts and feelings was unprecedented in 1959 and, even today, is a rare occurrence in the analytic literature. The word *marry* – such an ordinary word – is strangely powerful as a consequence of its connotations both of falling in love and of wishes to make a family and to live everyday life with the person one loves. It seems to me highly significant that the fantasies described by Searles never include imagining sexual intercourse (or any other explicit sexual activity) with the patient. I believe that this quality of Searles's fantasies reflects the nature of the conscious and unconscious fantasy life of the oedipal child. Although drawing this parallel between the analytic experience and the childhood experience is left largely to the reader, it seems to me that Searles is suggesting that for the oedipal boy, the idea of "marrying" his mother and being her "husband" are mysterious, ill-defined, and exciting ideas. To "marry" one's mother/patient is not so much a matter of having her as a sexual partner as it is a matter of having her all to oneself for one's entire life, having her as one's best friend and one's very beautiful, sexually exciting "wife" whom one deeply loves and one feels deeply loved by. Searles's writing does not make it clear to what degree these feelings and fantasies are conscious to Searles (or, by extension, to the oedipal child); that unclarity is, I believe, fully intended and reflects an aspect of the quality of Searles's (and perhaps the oedipal child's) emotional state while in the grips of oedipal love.

In this first clinical example, Searles describes feeling anxious, guilty, and embarrassed by his love for his patient. In response to the patient's saying that she felt sad about the imminent termination of the analysis, Searles said to her that he

> felt . . . much as did Mrs Gilbreth, of *Cheaper by the Dozen* fame, [who] . . . said to her husband, when the youngest of their twelve children was now passing out of the phase of early infancy, "It surely will be strange not to be waking up, for the first time in sixteen years, for the two-o'clock feeding!"
>
> (p. 290)

The patient looked "startled and murmured something about thinking that she had become older than that" (p. 290). Searles, in retrospect, came to understand that his focus on the patient's infantile needs represented an anxious retreat from his feelings of love for her as "an adult woman who could never be mine" (p. 290). Searles's fear of acknowledging to himself and (indirectly) to the patient his oedipal love (as opposed to the love of a parent for his or her infant) stemmed primarily from his fear that openly acknowledging such feelings would elicit attacks from his external and internal analytic elders:

> My training had been predominantly such as to make me hold rather suspect any strong feelings on the part of the analyst towards his patient, and these particular emotions [romantic and erotic wishes to marry the patient] seemed to be of an especially illegitimate nature.
>
> (p. 285)

Searles, even in this only partially successful management of oedipal love in the analytic setting, is implicitly raising an important question regarding his own experience of oedipal love for the patient. What is countertransference love as opposed to "non-countertransference" love? Is the former less real than the latter? If so, in what way? These questions are left unresolved for the time being.

As Searles, over the course of time, experienced oedipal love in the transference-countertransference as a consistent part of his analytic work, he says,

> I have grown successively less troubled at finding such responses in myself, less constrained to conceal these from the patient, and increasingly convinced that they augur well rather than ill for the outcome of our relationship, and that the patient's self-esteem benefits greatly from his sensing that he (or she) is capable of arousing such responses in his analyst. I have come to believe that there is a direct correlation between, on the one hand, the *affective intensity* with which the analyst experiences an awareness of such feelings – and of the unrealizability of such feelings – in himself towards the patient, and, on the other hand, the depth of maturation which the patient achieves in the analysis.
>
> (p. 291)

This passage illustrates the power of understatement in Searles's work. He leaves unspoken the central idea of the paper: *in order to successfully analyze the Oedipus complex, the analyst must fall in love with the patient while recognizing that his wishes will never be realized.* And, by extension, a successful oedipal experience in childhood requires that the oedipal parent fall deeply in love with the oedipal child while remaining fully aware that this love will never leave the domain of feelings. (In passages such as the one just cited, Searles seamlessly generates clinical theory from clinical description of the transference-countertransference.)

Searles's presentation of this first clinical example suggests an essential paradox underlying healthy oedipal love: both in childhood and in the transference-countertransference, the wished-for marriage is treated simultaneously as a real and as an imaginary marriage. There is at once the belief that the marriage is possible, and yet, at the same time, the knowledge (secured by the parents'/analyst's groundedness in their roles as parents/analyst) that the marriage is never to be. In the spirit of Winnicott's (1951) conception of "transitional object" relatedness, the question, "Does the analyst *really* want to marry his patient?" is never raised. The oedipal love of the patient and the analyst involves a state of mind suspended between reality and fantasy (see Gabbard, 1996, for a thoughtful examination and elaboration of this conception of transference-countertransference love).

The clinical examples that Searles provides in the remainder of his paper are all taken from work with chronic schizophrenic patients. Searles believes, on the basis of his extensive psychotherapeutic work at Chestnut Lodge, that the analysis of schizophrenic patients (and other patients suffering from psychological illnesses that have their origins in very early life) affords a particularly fruitful way of learning about the nature of experience that is common to all humankind. Searles believes that successful analytic work with such patients leads to an analytic relationship in which the most mature aspects of development (including the resolution of the Oedipus complex) are not only experienced and verbalized, but have a clarity and intensity, both in the transference and the countertransference, that is rare in work with healthier patients.

In discussing the analysis of a schizophrenic woman, Searles acknowledges that it was disconcerting to him, late in that analysis, to find himself feeling strong wishes to marry a woman "whom one's fellows might perceive as being . . . grossly ill and anything but attractive" (p. 292). But Searles's capacity to see his patient as a beautiful, highly desirable woman is precisely what was required of him. Searles found that straightforwardly facing his romantic feelings for this schizophrenic patient (while remaining clear in his own mind that he was the therapist) contributed to

> the resolution of what had become a stereotyped situation of the patient's being absorbed in making incestuous appeals to, or demands upon, the therapist, in a fashion which had been throttling the mutual investigation of the patient's difficulties . . . [W]hen . . . a therapist dare not even recognize such responses in himself – let alone expressing them to the patient – the situation tends all the more to remain stalemated at this level.
>
> (pp. 292–293)

Searles is suggesting here that the therapist's "candidly" (p. 292) allowing the patient to see that he or she stirs in him wishes to marry the patient does not have the effect of exacerbating the patient's unrelenting "incestuous appeals"; rather, the therapist's acknowledgment of "romantic love for the patient" contributes to the "resolution" of the stalemate (the repetitive, unrelenting incestuous appeals) and the "freeing-up" (p. 292) of the patient's and the therapist's capacities for analytic work. Though Searles does not discuss the theoretical underpinnings of his findings, it seems that the therapeutic effect of the expression of the therapist's love for the patient is being conceptualized not as a corrective emotional experience, but as the meeting of a developmental need for recognition of who the patient is (as opposed to the satisfying of an erotic desire). The latter would lead to increased sexual excitement; the former fosters psychological maturation, including the consolidation of a self that is experienced as both loved and loving. Searles is implicitly, and only implicitly, positing a human developmental need to love and be loved and to be recognized as a separate person whose love is valued.

Searles deepens his investigation into the role of the analyst's feelings of oedipal love of the patient by discussing a complex emotional situation that came to a head about eighteen months into the analysis of a "sensitive, highly intelligent, physically handsome" (p. 294) paranoid schizophrenic man. Searles began to feel uneasy about the intensity of his romantic feelings for this patient. He says he became alarmed during a session

> while we were sitting in silence and a radio not far away was playing a tenderly romantic song, when I realized that this man was dearer to me than anyone else in the world, including my wife. Within a few months I succeeded in finding "reality" reasons why I would not be able to continue indefinitely with his therapy, and he moved to a distant part of the country.
>
> (p. 294)

Searles hypothesizes that he had been able to tolerate the patient's sarcasm and scorn that replicated in the transference the patient's experience of feeling hated by his mother and, in return, feeling hateful toward her. What Searles had been unable "to brave" (p. 295) was the love in the transference-countertransference that had its origins in the love that had "prevailed [between the patient and his mother] behind a screen of mutual rejection" (p. 295). In particular, it was his romantic love for a man that frightened Searles so profoundly, at that early point in his career, that he was unable to continue working with this patient.

Searles's description of sitting with this patient while a radio was playing a tender love song never fails to stir me deeply. Searles does not simply tell the reader what occurred; he shows the reader what happened in the experience of reading: the tenderness of the music is created in the sound of the words. In the sentence describing this experience (cited above), the words "while we were" (three monosyllabic words repeating the soft "w" sound) are followed by "sitting in silence" (a pairing of two-syllable words beginning with a soft, sensuous "s" sound). The sentence continues to echo the soft "w" sounds of "while we were" in the words "away," "was," and "when," and ends with three tagged-on words that explode like a hand grenade: "including my wife." At the core of the denouement is the word "wife," which, with its own soft "w," conveys the feeling that this is the word that has been adumbrated all along, the word that has lain in wait in all that has preceded. The easy movement of sound creates in the experience of reading the tranquility of the love that Searles and the patient felt for one another, while the tagged-on thought, "including my wife," powerfully cuts through the dreamy quietude of the scene.

In this way, Searles creates in the experience of reading something of his experience of sudden, unexpected alarm at the juncture of the analysis being presented. The reader, too, is unprepared for this development and wonders if Searles could *really* mean what he says:

that the patient felt more dear to him than his wife. The compactness of the phrase, "including my wife," contributes to the unequivocal nature of the answer to this question: yes, he does mean it. And that fact so frightened Searles that he precipitated the premature end of the therapy. I believe that alarming surprises to the reader such as the one just described account for a good deal of the intense anger Searles was notorious for eliciting from audiences to whom he presented his work. Searles refuses to round the edges of an experience. Reading his work is not an experience of arriving at an understanding; it is an experience of being rudely woken up to disconcerting truths about one's experience with one's patients. Successive experiences of "waking up" to oneself on the part of the patient and analyst, for Searles, constitute a pivotal aspect of the analytic experience. It is when the therapist is not able to wake up to what is occurring that acting in and acting out (on the part of both the patient and the analyst) tend to occur. Here, too, these bits of clinical theory are implicit in Searles's descriptions of his clinical work.

In another analytic experience involving oedipal love for a man (which occurred some years after the clinical experience just described), Searles speaks of feeling a mixture of tender love and murderous hatred toward a severely ill paranoid-schizophrenic man:

> He referred to us, now in the third and fourth years of analysis, as being married . . . When I took him for a ride in my car for one of the sessions, I was amazed at the wholly delightful fantasy and feeling I had, namely that we were lovers on the threshold of marriage, with a whole world of wonders opening up before us; I had visions of going . . . to look for furniture together. . . .
>
> (p. 295)

The final detail of "going . . . to look for furniture together" poignantly conveys the excitement, not of sexual arousal, but of dreaming and planning a life to be lived with the person one loves. In oedipal love, these dreams on the part of both child and parent, patient and analyst, cannot be lived out with the current object of one's love: "I was filled with a poignant realization of how utterly and tragically unrealizable were the desires of this man who had been hospitalized continually, now, for fourteen years" (p. 296). In this second example of oedipal love for a man, Searles is saddened, not frightened, by his love for the patient. By this point in the paper, it comes as a surprise to me, but not as a shock, that Searles took for a ride in his car a patient for whom he was experiencing feelings of love and fantasies of being married. In reading this passage, I feel "amazed" (p. 295), to use Searles's word, not shocked or horrified by Searles's capacity to invent psychoanalysis anew for this patient. Not only has Searles grown emotionally in the course of the work that he has presented to this point, perhaps I, too, as reader, have matured in the course of the experience of reading his work.

For me, the paper builds toward a moment near its end when Searles speaks of his own experience as a parent and as a husband. I will quote this passage in its entirety because no paraphrase, no set of excerpts, can convey the effect created by the force of Searles's carefully chosen words:

> Not only my work with patients but also my experiences as a husband and a parent have convinced me of the validity of the current concepts which I am offering here. Towards my daughter, now eight years of age, I have experienced innumerable fantasies and feelings of a romantic-love kind, thoroughly complementary to the romantically adoring, seductive behaviour which she has shown towards her father oftentimes ever since she was about two or three years of age. I used at times to feel somewhat worried when she would play the supremely confident coquette with me and I would feel enthralled by her charms; but then I came to the conviction, some time ago, that such moments of relatedness could only be nourishing for her developing personality as well as delightful to me. If a little girl cannot feel herself able to win the heart of her father, her own father who has known her so well and for so long, and who is tied to her by mutual blood-ties, I reasoned, then how can the young woman who comes later have any deep confidence in the power of her womanliness?
>
> And I have every impression, similarly, that the oedipal desires of my son, now eleven years of age, have found a similarly lively and wholehearted feeling-response in my wife; and I am equally convinced that their deeply fond, openly evidenced mutual attraction is good for my son as well as enriching to my wife. To me it *makes sense* that the more a woman loves her husband, the more she will love, similarly, the lad who is, to at least a considerable degree, the younger edition of the man she loved enough to marry.
>
> (p. 296, my italics)

In this passage, Searles simply states, on the basis of his experience, what "makes sense" to him about the emotional effects that people have on one another. Simply saying what "makes sense" on the basis of one's experience – I cannot think of a better way of conveying the essential core of Searles's analytic thinking and way of practicing psychoanalysis.

The movement of the paper as a whole, and of this passage in particular, has the feel of a succession of photographs, each more skillfully crafted, each more successful in capturing the core of the subject being photographed: the analytic relationship. The words and images that are most alive for me in this passage – words and images that often come to my mind during analytic sessions – are the ones that Searles uses to describe the way his daughter, as a small child, could wrap him around her little finger: "If a little girl cannot feel herself able to win the heart of her father . . . then how can the young woman who comes later have any deep conviction in the power of her womanliness?" (p. 296). But, even as his daughter is sweeping him off his feet, Searles's wife, who earlier had stood in the shadows of his love for one of his patients, now takes her place in the mutual feeling of love that she and Searles experience, which is the source of the oedipal love that they feel for their children. In the very experience of writing and reading the paper, there is a movement from the experience of being enthralled with the person one (oedipally) loves to the "restitution" (Loewald, 1979, p. 393) of the parents' adult love for one another as the ballast for the oedipal experience.

As Searles's paper proceeds, the reader becomes increasingly aware of differences between Freud's (explicit) and Searles's (largely implicit) conceptions of the Oedipus complex. Searles points out that in Freud's (1900) earliest description of the Oedipus complex (in *The Interpretation of Dreams*), Freud "makes a fuller acknowledgement of the parents' participation in the oedipal phase of the child" (Searles, 1959, p. 297) than he does in any of his subsequent writings:

> The parents too give evidence as a rule of sexual partiality: a natural predilection usually sees to it that a man tends to spoil his little daughters while his wife takes her sons' part.
>
> (Freud, 1900, pp. 257–258; cited by Searles, 1959, p. 297)

Even this statement of the parents' oedipal love for the child is a pale rendering of what, in Searles's hands, is a vibrant, living thing that constitutes a good deal of the richness of human life, both for children and for parents. But this is not the heart of the difference between Searles's and Freud's conceptions of the Oedipus complex. For Freud (1910, 1921, 1923, 1924, 1925), the story of the healthy Oedipus complex is that of the child's triangulated sexual desire and romantic love for one parent, and his jealousy, intense rivalry, and murderous wishes for the other parent; the child's fearful and guilty renunciation (in the face of castration threats) of his sexual and romantic desires toward his parents; and the internalization of the threatening, punitive oedipal parents in the process of superego formation.

By contrast, Searles's version of the Oedipus complex is the story of the child's experience of reciprocated romantic and sexual love of the parent (a wish "to marry" and make a family and home with that parent). There is rivalry with, and jealousy of, the other parent, but it is a far quieter affair than that involved in Freud's conception of the child's murderous wishes for his parents. Searles's version of the oedipal experience does not end with the child's feeling defeated by castration threats and being left with an abiding sense of guilt and the need to renounce and ashamedly hide sexual and romantic wishes for the parent.

Instead, for Searles, the healthy Oedipus complex is the story of love and loss, of reciprocated romantic parent–child love that is safeguarded by the parents' firm but compassionate recognition of their roles, both as parents and as a couple. That recognition on the part of the parents helps the child (and the parents themselves) to accept the fact that this intense parent–child love relationship must be given up:

> The renunciation is, I think, again [like the reciprocation of the child's oedipal love] something which is a mutual experience for child and parent, and is made in deference to a recognizedly greater limiting reality, a reality which includes not only the taboo maintained by the rival-parent, but also the love of the oedipally desired parent towards his or her spouse – a love which antedated the child's birth and the love to which, in a sense, he owes his very existence.
>
> (p. 302)

In this rendering of the Oedipus complex, the child emerges with a feeling that his romantic and sexual love is accepted, valued, and reciprocated, along with a firm recognition of a "greater limiting reality" within which he must live. Both elements – the love and the loss – strengthen the child psychologically. The first element – the reciprocated oedipal love – enhances the child's feelings of self-worth. The second element – the loss involved in the ending of the oedipal romance – contributes to the child's sense of "a recognizedly greater limiting reality" (p. 302). This sense of a greater limiting reality involves an enhancement of the child's capacity to recognize and accept the unrealizability of his desires. This maturational step has far more to do with the maturation of reality testing and the capacity to differentiate internal and external reality than with the internalization of a chastising, threatening, punitive version of the parents (that is, superego formation). For Searles, the "heir" to the Oedipus complex is not primarily the formation of the superego, but a sense of oneself as a loving and lovable person who recognizes (with a feeling of loss) the constraints of external reality.

We can hear in this passage a partial response to the question raised earlier: "Is countertransference love, for Searles, less real than other kinds of love?" Clearly the answer is no. What makes countertransference love different from other types of love is the analyst's responsibility to recognize that the love that he experiences for and from the patient is an aspect of the analytic relationship, and to make use of his awareness of these feelings to further the therapeutic work in which he is engaged with the patient:

> These feelings [of love for the patient] come to him [the analyst] like all feelings, without tags showing whence they have come, and only if he is relatively open and accepting of their emergence into his awareness does he have a chance to set about finding out . . . their significance in his work with the patient.
>
> (pp. 300–301)

The notion that feelings come to the analyst "without tags" is pivotal to Searles's conception of oedipal love in the countertransference and to his overall conception of psychoanalysis. The analyst's task is first and foremost to allow himself to experience the full emotional intensity of *all that he feels in the here-and-now of the analytic experience.* Only then is he in a position to make analytic use of his feeling state.

## Unconscious identification

I will now turn to Searles's "Unconscious Identification" (1990), an important but little-known paper published in a collection of papers by fourteen analysts more than three decades after the "Oedipal Love" paper was published. The later paper reveals Searles's clinical thinking in its most highly developed form. There can be no doubt that the speaker in Searles's 1990 paper is the same person as the speaker in the 1959 paper, but now wiser, more artful in his work, more keenly aware of his limitations. In his 1990 paper, Searles is even more spare in his use of psychoanalytic theory than he was in the "Oedipal Love" paper. So far as I am able to discern, in his 1990 paper, Searles makes use of only two analytic theories: the concept of the dynamic unconscious and the concept of the transference-countertransference. The effect of Searles's paring away of theory to its absolute minimum is the creation of an experience in reading that is akin to reading fine literature: emotional situations are presented in which the characters involved are allowed to speak for themselves.

Searles begins the paper with a metaphor:

> My main purpose in this chapter is to convey a generous variety of clinical vignettes wherein one can detect unconscious identifications ramifying beneath or behind a relatively simple and obvious conscious one, something like a sea plant can be discovered to be flourishing far beyond and beneath the few leaves that can be seen on the water's surface.
>
> (1990, p. 211)

Searles lays out in this opening sentence his conception of how he views the relationship of conscious and unconscious experience in the analytic relationship. Conscious experience is "relatively simple and obvious," if one has developed an ear with which to notice it in oneself and frame it for oneself; "beneath or behind" conscious experience is unconscious experience which is continuous with conscious experience, just as the "flourishing," "ramifying" underwater parts of the sea plant are continuous with "the few leaves that can be seen at the water's surface." Implicit in this metaphor, as I read it, is the idea that one need not be a marine biologist to notice a few of the qualities of the sea plant, but the more one's mind and senses are capable of refined perception, the more one is likely to understand about the way the plant works and how it has come to work in that way. Moreover, a person with a trained eye is also more likely to feel curious, puzzled, and amazed by what he or she observes. And yet, as I hope to show in the course of my discussion of this paper, Searles's use of this metaphor fails to capture what is most important about Searles's way of thinking and working.

In the first of the clinical illustrations, Searles describes his work with an elderly woman who for many years had not heard from her daughter. Having received a letter from her daughter (then in her 40s), the patient brought the letter to the session, not certain how to reply to it. She gave it to Searles to read. On thinking about it, Searles said, "I do feel a sense of not actually being you, and therefore, I feel uncomfortable as to how I might respond to it" (p. 214). A bit later, Searles conversationally addresses the reader:

> Actually, for me, the most memorable aspect of this interaction is that, in the moment before reaching out to accept the letter, I felt a very strong sense that it was not right for me to read the letter, since *I* was not the person to whom the letter was addressed; the force of this inhibition was striking to me, in light of her obvious wish that I read it.
>
> It then occurred to me, as I went on talking, and I said, "But I wonder if *you* feel that *you*, likewise, are not the person to whom that letter is addressed." To this, she reacted in a strongly confirmatory fashion, saying that she had gotten a great deal of therapy over the years since she had been involved in the kind of thing that this letter was expressing. In essence, she strongly confirmed that my sense of not in actuality being the intended recipient of the letter had a counterpart in her strongly feeling, likewise, that she was not the person to whom the letter was addressed. Her confirmation, here, was expressed in sufficiently pent-up feeling as to let me know that she had needed this interpretation from me to enable her to know and express these feelings so clearly.
>
> (pp. 214–215, italics in original)

The analytic event being presented hinges on Searles's awareness in the moment before he reached out to accept the letter that he felt uncomfortable with the idea of reading a letter that was not written to him. On the basis of this feeling/thought, Searles did something with the situation that, for me, is astounding: he turned the experience "inside out" in his mind in a way that revealed something that felt true to him, to the patient, and to me, as a reader. (With regard to my use of the metaphor of turning experience inside out, it is important to bear in mind that, like the surface of a Möbius strip, inside is continually in the process of becoming outside and outside becoming inside.) Searles took his feeling that it was not right to read a letter not addressed to him – the "inside," in the sense that it was his own personal response – and made it "the outside." By "outside," I mean the context, the larger emotional reality, within which he was experiencing what was occurring between himself and the patient and, by extension, within which the patient was experiencing herself in relation to her daughter. It is precisely this sort of reversal that is most surprising, often startling, about the experience of reading Searles: there is an abrupt shift from Searles's inner life (his extraordinarily perceptive emotional response to what is occurring) to the invisible psychological context within which the patient is experiencing himself or herself.

The reversal to which I am referring is not synonymous with making the unconscious conscious. What Searles does is far more subtle than that. In this example, the patient's experience of no longer being the person her daughter imagines her to be is not a repressed unconscious thought and feeling; rather, it is part of the internal emotional environment in which the patient lives. That as-yet-unnamed matrix of her self had come to constitute a good deal of the truth of who she had become. In the interaction described, it was necessary, first, for Searles to make a transformation within himself in which context became content: the "invisible" context of Searles's sense of himself (as not being the person to whom the letter was written) became the "visible," thinkable content. Searles, in the process of thinking out loud, came to the feeling/idea that the patient did not experience herself as the person to whom the letter was written: "It then occurred to me, as I went on talking . . ." (p. 214). Searles was not saying what he thought; he was thinking what he said. That is, in the very act of speaking, inner was becoming outer, thinking was becoming talking, unthinkable context was becoming thinkable content, experience was being turned inside out.

I will now turn to another example of Searles turning experience inside out. In a clinical discussion later in the paper, he recounts instances of being asked by patients, "How are you?" Searles describes often feeling

> that I would dearly love to be able to unburden myself, and tell him in . . . detail of the myriad aspects of how I am feeling today; but knowing how impossible this is, in light of our true situation here, I react mainly with bitterly ironic amusement saying, "Just grand," or merely nodding.
>
> (p. 216)

It eventually occurs to Searles, each time freshly and unexpectedly, that the patient is feeling something very similar to Searles's feelings – that is, that it is impossible under the circumstances to tell Searles how he (the patient) feels. This is so because "*he* [the patient] is [feeling that he is] supposed to be the one who is helping *me*" (p. 216), as was the case in the patient's childhood relationship with his parents. When Searles comes to this type of understanding of the situation, he remains silent and yet his grasp of what is occurring "nonetheless enables me . . . to foster an atmosphere wherein the patient can feel that he is being met with more of genuine patience and empathy than had been the case before" (p. 216).

In this clinical situation, Searles realizes that a critical aspect of the context of his emotional experience of being the analyst for his patient has been his (Searles's) wish to be the patient in the analysis. His hearing the bitterness in his own voice as he responds to the patient's question/invitation makes it possible for him to convert unthinkable context into thinkable content. This transformation allows Searles to communicate (nonverbally) an understanding of the patient's invisible (silent) bitterness about the fact that he does not feel that he has the right to be the patient in his own analysis. Here, again, Searles does the psychological work of transforming his own "inner" emotional context (his wish that the analysis were his analysis) into "outer" (thinkable, verbally symbolized) thoughts and feelings. This psychological work on Searles's part contributes to a change in the "atmosphere" of the analytic relationship. The formerly unthinkable context for the patient's experience (his sense that the analysis was not *his* analysis) enters a process of being consciously thought by Searles and unconsciously thought by the patient.

I will take a piece of Searles's self-analytic work as a final illustration of the way in which his thinking is, to a great extent, marked by his unique way of turning experience inside out:

> For many years I have enjoyed washing dishes, and not rarely have

> had the feeling that this is the one thing in my life that I feel entirely comfortably capable of doing. I have always assumed that, in my washing of dishes, I was identifying with my mother, who routinely did them in my early childhood. But in recent years . . . it has occurred to me that I have been identifying with my mother not only in the form but also in my spirit of washing the dishes. I had not previously allowed myself to consider the possibility that she, too, may have felt so chronically overwhelmed, so chronically out beyond her depth in life, that this activity, this washing of dishes, was the one part of her life with which she felt fully equipped to cope comfortably.
>
> (p. 224)

This paragraph could have been written by no one other than Searles – in part because it involves such exquisite mastery of the art of looking deeply *into* seemingly ordinary conscious experience. Searles knows in a way that few analysts have known that there is only one consciousness and that the unconscious aspect of consciousness is *in* the conscious aspect, not under it or behind it. Paradoxically, Searles knows this in practice and makes use of it in virtually every clinical illustration he presents, but he has not, as far as I am aware, ever discussed this conception of consciousness in his writing. Moreover, in the opening sentence of the paper cited earlier, Searles explicitly contradicts this understanding of the relationship of conscious and unconscious experience when he says that unconscious identifications lie "behind and beneath" conscious identifications. This conception of the relationship between conscious and unconscious experience (and the accompanying sea-plant metaphor) are not in keeping with the understanding of the relationship between conscious and unconscious experience that Searles so powerfully illustrates in this paper. I believe that it would more accurately reflect what Searles demonstrates in his clinical work to say that conscious and unconscious experience are qualities of a unitary consciousness, and that we gain access to the unconscious dimension of experience by looking *into* conscious experience, not by looking "behind" it or "beneath" it.

In the account of his psychological state while washing dishes, Searles had for years thought of his enjoyment of washing dishes and his feeling that that is the "one thing in my life that I feel entirely comfortably capable of doing" as an identification in the "form," but not in the "spirit," of his mother washing dishes. The reader (and Searles) is taken by surprise as Searles delves more deeply into his experience of washing dishes. He becomes aware of what he already "knew," but did not know: his experience of washing dishes takes place within a powerful, yet invisible, emotional context of feelings of profound inadequacy. Searles transforms this formerly unthinkable context into thinkable emotional content:

> I had not previously allowed myself to consider the possibility that she, too, may have felt so chronically overwhelmed, so chronically out beyond her depth in life, that this activity, this washing of dishes, was the one part of her life with which she felt fully equipped to cope comfortably.
>
> (p. 224)

The truth (and even beauty) of Searles's newly created understanding of himself and his mother is not merely described for the reader, it is shown to the reader in the evocativeness of the imagery. The image of Searles as a child watching his mother with a sink full of dishes in soapy water not only captures the experience of the day-to-day life of a boy with his depressed mother; it also conveys a sense of the emotional shallowness (the very limited depth of a kitchen sink) beyond which his mother dared not – could not – go.

## Searles and Bion

I will conclude by briefly discussing a complementarity between Searles's thinking and that of Bion that I "discovered" to my surprise in the course of writing this chapter. Searles was temperamentally disinclined (and perhaps unable) to formulate his thoughts at a level of abstraction beyond that of clinical theory. In stark contrast, Bion, whose focus was on the development of psychoanalytic theory, gives the reader very little sense of the way in which he makes use of his ideas in the analytic setting. In a highly condensed way, I will address three aspects of the work of Searles and Bion in which I suggest that the reader requires familiarity with the work of both authors in order to fully appreciate either one.

## *The container-contained*

In discussing Searles's way of working with his patient's request that he read a letter written to her by her daughter, I introduced the idea that Searles's thinking might be thought of as "turning experience inside out" – what begins as the invisible, unthinkable context of experience is transformed by Searles into experiential content, about which he and the patient may be able to think and talk. My metaphoric description of what Searles was doing (without my being aware of it) drew on Bion's (1962a) concept of the container-contained. The concept of the container-contained provides a way of thinking about the way in which psychological content (thoughts and feelings) may overwhelm and destroy the very capacity for thinking thoughts (the container) (see Chapter 6 and Ogden, 2004c, for discussions of Bion's concept of the container-contained). Searles's patient may have harbored feelings of guilt of such intensity that they limited her capacity to think her thoughts concerning the ways in which she had changed, thus leaving her without the means to do unconscious psychological work with them. Searles was able to think (contain) something like the patient's unthinkable thoughts concerning his own guilt/uneasiness about the idea of reading a letter not addressed to him. In telling the patient that he thought that she, too, did not experience herself as the person to whom the letter was written, Searles helped the patient to contain/think her own previously unthinkable thoughts and feelings concerning the psychological growth that she had achieved.

In formulating Searles's work in this way, I am creating a vantage point that is lacking in Searles's work – that is, a conception of the way in which the analytic interaction involves at every turn the muscular interplay of thoughts and the capacity to think one's thoughts. At the same time, Searles's extraordinary capacity to describe the emotional shifts occurring in the transference-countertransference brings to life the experiential level of the workings of the container-contained in ways that, to my mind, Bion was unable to achieve in his own writing.

## *The human need for truth*

Searing honesty (with himself and with the patient) permeates Searles's accounts of his clinical work. Examples discussed in this chapter that come immediately to mind include Searles's acknowledging to himself (despite internal and external pressures to do otherwise) his intense wishes to marry his patients when in the thick of oedipal transference-countertransference experiences; Searles's alarming awareness that he felt a depth of tenderness toward a male schizophrenic patient that was greater than the love he felt for his wife; and his recognition of his feelings of bitterness about the fact that he was not the patient in the analysis that he was conducting and, consequently, did not have the right to tell the patient at length what he was feeling. While Searles clearly believes that straightforwardly facing the truth of what is occurring in the analytic relationship is an indispensable element in analytic work, it took Bion to formulate this clinical awareness at a higher level of abstraction – namely, that the most fundamental principle of human motivation is the need to know the truth about one's lived emotional experience. "[T]he welfare of the patient demands a constant supply of truth as inevitably as his physical survival demands food" (Bion, 1992, p. 99; see also Chapter 6). Searles is without peer in demonstrating what that need for truth looks like and feels like in the transference-countertransference and how it shapes the analytic experience; Bion put the idea into words, located it in relation to analytic theory as a whole, and created an understanding of the human condition that placed the need for truth at its core.

### *Reconceiving the relationship of conscious and unconscious experience*

It is evident in Searles's descriptions of his analytic work that the relationship of the analyst's conscious and unconscious experience is being conceived of quite differently from the way in which that interplay is ordinarily conceptualized. Though not stated explicitly, Searles shows the reader what it means to make use of consciousness as a whole – that is, to create conditions in the analytic setting in which the analyst perceives what is occurring in the transference-countertransference by means of a form of consciousness characterized by a seamless continuity of conscious and unconscious experience. Bion recognized in his own work what Searles demonstrates in his clinical accounts, and used that recognition to revolutionize analytic theory by radically altering the topographic model. Bion's alteration of the topographic model is nothing less than breathtaking in that it had been impossible, at least for me, to imagine psychoanalysis without the idea of an unconscious mind somehow separate from ("below") the conscious mind. The conscious and unconscious "minds," for Bion, are not separate entities, but dimensions of a single consciousness. The apparent separateness of the conscious and unconscious mind is, for Bion (1962a), merely an artifact of the vantage point from which we observe and think about human experience. In other words, consciousness and unconsciousness are aspects of a single entity viewed from different vertices. The unconscious is always a dimension of consciousness whether or not it is easily perceptible, just as the stars are always in the sky whether or not they are obscured by the glare of the sun.

Bion (1962a) developed his concept of "reverie" (a state of receptivity to one's own and the patient's conscious/unconscious experience) concurrently with Searles's early descriptions (written in the 1950s and 1960s) of his work with chronic schizophrenic patients in which he makes use of a state of mind that blurs the distinction between conscious and unconscious aspects of experience. It is impossible to say to what extent Bion was influenced by Searles, or Searles by Bion. Searles makes reference only to Bion's relatively early work on projective identification; Bion makes no reference at all to Searles's work. Nonetheless, what I hope to have demonstrated is that Searles's work is enriched conceptually by a knowledge of Bion's work, and Bion's work is brought more fully to life experientially by a familiarity with Searles's work.

# References


Anderson, A. and McLaughlin, F. (1963) Some observations on psychoanalytic supervision. *Psychoanalytic Quarterly*, 32: 77–93.

Baudry, F. D. (1993) The personal dimension and management of the supervisory situation with a special note on the parallel process. *Psychoanalytic Quarterly*, 62: 588–614.

Berger, J. and Mohr, J. (1967) *A Fortunate Man: The Story of a Country Doctor*. New York: Pantheon.

Berman, E. (2000) Psychoanalytic supervision: The intersubjective development. *International Journal of Psychoanalysis*, 81: 273–290.

Bion, W. R. (1948–1951) Experiences in groups. In *Experiences in Groups and Other Papers* (pp. 27–137). New York: Basic Books, 1959.

Bion, W. R. (1952) Group dynamics: A review. *International Journal of Psychoanalysis*, 33: 235–247.

Bion, W. R. (1957) Differentiation of the psychotic from the non-psychotic personalities. In *Second Thoughts* (pp. 43–64). New York: Aronson, 1967.

Bion, W. R. (1959) *Experiences in Groups and Other Papers*. New York: Basic Books.

Bion, W. R. (1962a) *Learning from Experience*. In *Seven Servants*. New York: Aronson, 1975.

Bion, W. R. (1962b) A theory of thinking. In *Second Thoughts* (pp. 110–119). New York: Aronson.

Bion, W. R. (1963) *Elements of Psycho-Analysis*. In *Seven Servants*. New York: Aronson, 1975.

Bion, W. R. (1967) Notes on the theory of schizophrenia. In *Second Thoughts* (pp. 23–35). New York: Aronson.

Bion, W. R. (1970) *Attention and Interpretation*. In *Seven Servants*. New York: Aronson, 1975.

Bion, W. R. (1987) Clinical seminars. In F. Bion (ed.), *Clinical Seminars and Other Works* (pp. 1–240). London: Karnac.

Bion, W. R. (1992) *Cogitations*, F. Bion (ed.). London: Karnac.

Borges, J. L. (1923) *Fervor de Buenos Aires*. Privately printed. Excerpts in English in *Jorge L. Borges: Selected Poems*, A. Coleman (ed.) (pp. 1–32). New York: Viking, 1999.

Borges, J. L. (1962) Kafka and his precursors. In J. Irby (trans.) and D. Yates and J. Irby (eds.), *Labyrinths: Selected Stories and Other Writings* (pp. 199–201). New York: New Directions.

Borges, J. L. (1970a) Preface. In N. T. Di Giovanni (trans.), *Dr Brodie's Report* (pp. 11–14). London: Penguin, 1976.

Borges, J. L. (1970b) An autobiographical essay. In N. T. Di Giovanni (ed. and trans.), *The Aleph and Other Stories, 1933–1969* (pp. 203–262). New York: Dutton.

Borges, J. L. (1980) *Seven Nights*, E. Weinberger (trans.). New York: New Directions, 1984.

Borges, J. L. (1984) *Twenty-Four Conversations with Borges (Including a Selection of Poems). Interviews with Roberto Alifano 1981–1983*, N. S. Arauz, W. Barnstone and N. Escandell (trans.). Housatonic, MA: Lascaux Publishers.

Breuer, J. and Freud, S. (1893–1895) *Studies on Hysteria*. SE 2. (*The Standard Edition of the Complete Psychological Works of Sigmund Freud*. J. Strachey [ed. and trans.]. London: Hogarth Press, 1974.)

Chodorow, N. (2003) The psychoanalytic vision of Hans Loewald. *International Journal of Psychoanalysis*, 84: 897–913.

Chomsky, N. (1968) *Language and Mind*. New York: Harcourt, Brace and World.

Coetzee, J. M. (1983) *Life & Times of Michael K*. New York: Penguin.

Coetzee, J. M. (1990) *The Age of Iron*. New York: Penguin.

Coetzee, J. M. (1999) *Disgrace*. New York: Penguin.

Davis, L. (2007) What you learn about the baby. In *Varieties of Disturbance* (pp. 115–124). New York: Farrar, Straus and Giroux.

DeLillo, D. (1997) *Underworld*. New York: Scribner.

de M' Uzan, M. (2003) Slaves of quantity. *Psychoanalytic Quarterly*, 72: 711–725. ([1984] Les esclaves de la quantité. *Nouvelle Revue Psychanalyse*, 30: 129–138.)

Doehrman, M. J. (1976) Parallel processes in supervision and psychotherapy. *Bulletin of the Menninger Clinic*, 40: 3–104.

Epstein, L. (1986) Collusive selective inattention to the negative impact of the supervisory interaction. *Contemporary Psychoanalysis*, 22: 389–409.

Freud, S. (1900) *The Interpretation of Dreams*. SE 4–5.

Freud, S. (1905) Three essays on the theory of sexuality. SE 7.

Freud, S. (1909) Analysis of a phobia in a five-year-old. SE 10.

Freud, S. (1910) A special type of object choice made by men (Contributions to a psychology of love I). SE 11.

Freud, S. (1911) Formulations on the two principles of mental functioning. SE 12.

Freud, S. (1916–1917) *Introductory Lectures on Psycho-Analysis*. SE 15–16.

Freud, S. (1917) Mourning and melancholia. SE 14.

Freud, S. (1921) *Group Psychology and the Analysis of the Ego*. SE 18.

Freud, S. (1923) *The Ego and the Id*. SE 19.

Freud, S. (1924) The dissolution of the Oedipus complex. SE 19.

Freud, S. (1925) Some psychical consequences of the anatomical distinction between the sexes. SE 19.

Frost, R. (1939) The figure a poem makes. In R. Poirier and M. Richardson (eds.), *Robert Frost: Collected Poems, Prose and Plays* (pp. 776–778). New York: Library of America, 1995.

Frost, R. (1942) Never again would birds' song be the same. In R. Poirier and M. Richardson (eds.), *Robert Frost: Collected Poems, Prose and Plays* (p. 308). New York: Library of America, 1995.

Gabbard, G. O. (1996) *Love and Hate in the Analytic Setting*. Northvale, NJ: Aronson.

Gabbard, G. O. (1997a) The psychoanalyst at the movies. *International Journal of Psychoanalysis*, 78: 429–434.

Gabbard, G. O. (1997b) Neil Jordan's *The Crying Game. International Journal of Psychoanalysis*, 78: 825–828.

Gabbard, G. O. (2007) "Bound in a nutshell": Thoughts about complexity, reductionism and "infinite space". *International Journal of Psychoanalysis*, 88: 559–574.

Gabbard, G. O. and Gabbard, K. (1999) *Psychiatry and the Cinema* (2nd ed.). Washington, DC: American Psychiatric Press.

Gabbard, G. O. and Lester, E. (1995) *Boundaries and Boundary Violations in Psychoanalysis*. New York: Basic Books.

Gediman, H. K. and Wolkenfeld, F. (1980) The parallelism phenomenon in psychoanalysis and supervision: Its reconsideration as a triadic system. *Psychoanalytic Quarterly*, 49: 234–255.

Gould, G. (1974) *Glenn Gould: The Alchemist*. (A documentary film by B. Monsaingeon). EMI Archive Film.

Grotstein, J. S. (2000) *Who is the Dreamer who Dreams the Dream? A Study of Psychic Presences*. Hillsdale, NJ: Analytic Press.

Grotstein, J. S. (2007) *A Beam of Intense Darkness: Wilfred Bion's Legacy to Psychoanalysis*. London: Karnac.

Karp, G. and Berrill, N. J. (1981) *Development* (2nd ed.). New York: McGraw-Hill.

Kaywin, R. (1993) The theoretical contributions of Hans W. Loewald. *Psychoanalytic Study of the Child*, 48: 99–114.

Klein, M. (1946) Notes on some schizoid mechanisms. In *Envy and Gratitude and Other Works, 1946–1963* (pp. 1–24). New York: Delacorte Press/Seymour Laurence, 1975.

Langs, R. (1979) *The Supervisory Experience*. New York: Aronson.

Laplanche, J. and Pontalis, J.-B. (1967) Repression. In D. N. Smith (trans.), *The Language of Psychoanalysis* (pp. 390–394). New York: Norton, 1973.

Lesser, R. (1984) Supervision: Illusions, anxieties and questions. In L. Caligor, P. M. Bromberg, and J. D. Meltzer (eds.), *Clinical Perspectives on the Supervision of Psychoanalysis and Psychotherapy* (pp. 143–152). New York: Plenium, 1984.

Loewald, H. (1979) The waning of the Oedipus complex. In *Papers on Psychoanalysis* (pp. 384–404). New Haven, CT: Yale University Press, 1980.

McDougall, J. (1984) The "dis-affected" patient: Reflections on affect pathology. *Psychoanalytic Quarterly*, 53: 386–409.

McKinney, M. (2000) Relational perspectives and the supervisory triad. *Psychoanalytic Psychology*, 17: 565–584.

Meltzer, D. (1983) *Dream-Life*. Perthshire, Scotland: Clunie Press.

Mitchell, S. (1998) From ghosts to ancestors: The psychoanalytic vision of Hans Loewald. *Psychoanalytic Dialogues*, 8: 825–855.

Ogden, T. H. (1979) On projective identification. *International Journal of Psychoanalysis*, 60: 357–373.

Ogden, T. H. (1980) On the nature of schizophrenic conflict. *International Journal of Psychoanalysis*, 61: 513–533.

Ogden, T. H. (1982) *Projective Identification and Psychotherapeutic Technique*. New York: Jason Aronson/London: Karnac.

Ogden, T. H. (1986a) *The Matrix of the Mind: Object Relations and the Psychoanalytic Dialogue*. Northvale, NJ: Aronson/London: Karnac.

Ogden, T. H. (1986b) Instinct, phantasy and psychological deep structure in the work of Melanie Klein. In *The Matrix of the Mind: Object Relations and the Psychoanalytic Dialogue* (pp. 9–39). Northvale, NJ: Aronson/London: Karnac.

Ogden, T. H. (1987) The transitional oedipal relationship in female development. *International Journal of Psychoanalysis*, 68: 485–498.

Ogden, T. H. (1989a) The schizoid condition. In *The Primitive Edge of Experience* (pp. 83–108). Northvale, NJ: Aronson/London: Karnac.

Ogden, T. H. (1989b) The concept of an autistic-contiguous position. *International Journal of Psychoanalysis*, 70: 127–140.

Ogden, T. H. (1989c) *The Primitive Edge of Experience*. Northvale, NJ: Aronson/London: Karnac.

Ogden, T. H. (1994) The analytic third – working with intersubjective clinical facts. *International Journal of Psychoanalysis*, 75: 3–20.

Ogden, T. H. (1997a) Reverie and interpretation. *Psychoanalytic Quarterly*, 66: 567–595.

Ogden, T. H. (1997b) *Reverie and Interpretation: Sensing Something Human.* Northvale, NJ: Aronson/London: Karnac.

Ogden, T. H. (1997c) Listening: Three Frost poems. *Psychoanalytic Dialogues*, 7: 619–639.

Ogden, T. H. (1997d) Some thoughts on the use of language in psychoanalysis. *Psychoanalytic Dialogues*, 7: 1–21.

Ogden, T. H. (1998) A question of voice in poetry and psychoanalysis. *Psychoanalytic Quarterly*, 67: 426–448.

Ogden, T. H. (1999) "The music of what happens" in poetry and psychoanalysis. *International Journal of Psychoanalysis*, 80: 979–994.

Ogden, T. H. (2000) Borges and the art of mourning. *Psychoanalytic Dialogues*, 10: 65–88.

Ogden, T. H. (2001a) Reading Winnicott. *Psychoanalytic Quarterly*, 70: 279–323.

Ogden, T. H. (2001b) An elegy, a love song and a lullaby. *Psychoanalytic Dialogues*, 11: 293–311.

Ogden, T. H. (2002) A new reading of the origins of object-relations theory. *International Journal of Psychoanalysis*, 83: 767–782.

Ogden, T. H. (2003a) On not being able to dream. *International Journal of Psychoanalysis*, 84: 17–30.

Ogden, T. H. (2003b) What's true and whose idea was it? *International Journal of Psychoanalysis*, 84: 593–606.

Ogden, T. H. (2004a) This art of psychoanalysis: Dreaming undreamt dreams and interrupted cries. *International Journal of Psychoanalysis*, 85: 857–877.

Ogden, T. H. (2004b) An introduction to the reading of Bion. *International Journal of Psychoanalysis*, 85: 285–300.

Ogden, T. H. (2004c) On holding and containing, being and dreaming. *International Journal of Psychoanalysis*, 85: 1349–1364.

Ogden, T. H. (2005a) *This Art of Psychoanalysis: Dreaming Undreamt Dreams and Interrupted Cries.* (New Library of Psychoanalysis.) London and New York: Routledge.

Ogden, T. H. (2005b) On psychoanalytic writing. *International Journal of Psychoanalysis*, 86: 15–29.

Plato (1997) *Phaedrus*. In J. M. Cooper (ed.), *Plato: Complete Works* (pp. 506–556). Indianapolis, IN: Hackett.

Poe, E. A. (1848) To —— . In *The Complete Tales and Poems of Edgar Allan Poe* (p. 80). New York: Barnes and Noble, 1992.

Pritchard, W. H. (1994) Ear training. In *Playing It by Ear: Literary Essays and Reviews* (pp. 3–18). Amherst, MA: University of Massachusetts Press.

Sandler, J. (1976) Dreams, unconscious fantasies and 'identity of perception'. *International Review of Psychoanalysis*, 3: 33–42.

Searles, H. (1955) The informational value of the supervisor's emotional experiences. In *Collected Papers on Schizophrenia and Related Subjects* (pp. 157–176). New York: International Universities Press, 1965.

Searles, H. (1959) Oedipal love in the countertransference. In *Selected Papers on Schizophrenia and Related Subjects* (pp. 284–303). New York: International Universities Press, 1965.

Searles, H. (1990) Unconscious identification. In L. B. Boyer and P. Giovacchini (eds.), *Master Clinicians: On Treating the Regressed Patient* (pp. 211–226). Northvale, NJ: Aronson.

Slavin, J. (1998) Influence and vulnerability in psychoanalytic supervision and treatment. *Psychoanalytic Psychology*, 15: 230–244.

Springmann, R. R. (1986) Countertransference clarification in supervision. *Contemporary Psychoanalysis*, 22: 252–277.

Stimmel, B. (1995) Resistance to the awareness of the supervisor's transference with special reference to parallel process. *International Journal of Psychoanalysis*, 76: 609–618.

Tower, L. E. (1956) Countertransference. *Journal of the American Psychoanalytic Association*, 4: 224–255.

Tustin, F. (1981) *Autistic States in Children*. Boston: Routledge and Kegan Paul.

Weinstein, A. (1998) Audio tape 1. In *Classics in American Literature*. Chantilly, VA: Teaching Company.

Williams, W. C. (1984a) *The Doctor Stories*. New York: New Directions.

Williams, W. C. (1984b) The girl with a pimply face. In *The Doctor Stories* (pp. 42–55). New York: New Directions.

Williams, W. C. (1984c) The use of force. In *The Doctor Stories* (pp. 56–60). New York: New Directions.

Winnicott, D. W. (1945) Primitive emotional development. In *Through Paediatrics to Psycho-Analysis* (pp. 145–156). New York: Basic Books, 1975.

Winnicott, D. W. (1947) Hate in the countertransference. In *Through Paediatrics to Psycho-Analysis* (pp. 194–203). New York: Basic Books, 1975.

Winnicott, D. W. (1951) Transitional objects and transitional phenomena. In *Playing and Reality* (pp. 1–25). New York: Basic Books, 1971.

Winnicott, D. W. (1956) Primary maternal preoccupation. In *Through Paediatrics to Psycho-Analysis* (pp. 300–305). New York: International Universities Press, 1975.

Winnicott, D. W. (1960) The theory of the parent–infant relationship. In *The Maturational Processes and the Facilitating Environment* (pp. 33–55). New York: International Universities Press, 1965.

Winnicott, D. W. (1964) *The Infant, the Child and the Outside World.* Baltimore, MD: Pelican.

Winnicott, D. W. (1968) The use of an object and relating through identifications. In *Playing and Reality* (pp. 86–94). New York: Basic Books, 1971.

Winnicott, D. W. (1971) Playing: A theoretical statement. In *Playing and Reality* (pp. 38–52). New York: Basic Books.

Wolkenfeld, F. (1990) The parallel process phenomenon revisited: Some additional thoughts about the supervisory process. In R. C. Lane (ed.), *Psychoanalytic Approaches to Supervision* (pp. 95–109). New York: Brunner/Mazel.

Yerushalmi, H. (1992) On the concealment of the interpersonal therapeutic reality in the course of supervision. *Psychotherapy*, 29: 438–446.

# Index